ISBN 978-1-334-39973-2
PIBN 10740595

English
Français
Deutsche
Italiano
Español
Português

www.forgottenbooks.com

Mythology Photography **Fiction**
Fishing Christianity **Art** Cooking
Essays Buddhism Freemasonry
Medicine **Biology** Music **Ancient
Egypt** Evolution Carpentry Physics
Dance Geology **Mathematics** Fitness
Shakespeare **Folklore** Yoga Marketing
Confidence Immortality Biographies
Poetry **Psychology** Witchcraft
Electronics Chemistry History **Law**
Accounting **Philosophy** Anthropology
Alchemy Drama Quantum Mechanics
Atheism Sexual Health **Ancient History**
Entrepreneurship Languages Sport
Paleontology Needlework Islam
Metaphysics Investment Archaeology
Parenting Statistics Criminology
Motivational

BALABISH

BY

G. A. WAINWRIGHT

WITH A PREFACE BY

T. WHITTEMORE

WITH TWENTY-FIVE PLATES

THIRTY-SEVENTH MEMOIR OF

THE EGYPT EXPLORATION SOCIETY

PUBLISHED UNDER THE DIRECTION OF THE COMMITTEE

LONDON:

GEORGE ALLEN & UNWIN, LTD.

RUSKIN HOUSE, 40, MUSEUM STREET, W.C.

1920

LONDON :

PRINTED BY WILLIAM CLOWES AND SONS, LIMITED,
DUKE STREET, STAMFORD STREET, S.E.

EGYPT EXPLORATION SOCIETY

President

GENERAL THE RT. HON. SIR JOHN MAXWELL, G.C.B., K.C.M.G.,

Vice=Presidents

W 75040

PREFACE.

By Professor THOMAS WHITTEMORE.

AT the close of the season of 1914, at Abydos, Mr. G. A. Wainwright and I turned to a special concession granted to the Egypt Exploration Society by the Department of Antiquities, in response to a request of the American branch of the Society for objects for a group of small American museums.

The site included Sawama and Balabish. Both had been previously excavated by the Department of Antiquities, as well as frequently plundered by natives, but it was thought that they might still yield types of pottery much sought by the museums, and, perhaps, other objects of interest.

Work was begun at Sawama with about twenty men and twice as many boys. An interesting Eighteenth Dynasty cemetery was found here, consisting chiefly of burials of women. Although few of these burials were undisturbed, many objects remained, beautifully to characterize the jewellers' art of the time. Among the objects were bracelets of ebony and ivory, and a necklace of exquisite silver ornaments in the form of flies; ivory wands, carved with the head of Hathor, delicate portrait reliefs in plaster, toilet articles in lapis lazuli, blue glass, ivory, wood and tortoise-shell. The pottery, largely Syrian or Syrianizing, presented many charming and some rare forms. The cemetery was rich in scarabs of Amenophis I, Tuthmosis III, and Amenophis III.

The excavation at Balabish, fifty miles south of Sawama, on the same side of the river, carried out by Mr. Wainwright and myself in the winter of 1915, was the only excavation undertaken by the Society during the war.

At Balabish we found the site to be mainly of the New Kingdom and later. The burials, though plundered, yielded objects of considerable interest and of distinct museum value. But the discovery of signal importance here was a small group of pan-graves.

The graves of this group lay adjoining one another, on desert promontories at the ends nearest the cultivation. The graves were not shallow and pan-shaped, but of the deeper well-shaped variety, from 1½ to 2 metres deep. Typical pan-grave objects were also found in oblong graves so small as often to suggest crouched burials, and in full length rectangular graves of the usual Egyptian type.

Among the contents of these graves were ceremonially broken _kohl_-pots, bronze axe-heads, jars of scented ointment, finely worked leather—presumably in the form of garments—dyed and with pierced and tooled ornamentation, shell bracelets, bow-strings, leather wrist-guards, and an exceptionally interesting bag woven of giraffe's hair. There was an abundance of well-polished pottery, both plain and with metallic black rim, as well as fine, dull red ware in the form of bowls with incised ornamentation.

Thus it will be seen that these burials present the two fold, little-known life of this belated people, who, leaving the backwaters of the South, came bearing lingering pre-dynastic tradition into the new civilization of the Middle Kingdom.

In the present volume it has been found possible to publish only an account of the work at Balabish. It is written entirely by Mr. Wainwright from our notes and from the card catalogue in his possession, and has been seen through the Press by the officers of the Society The drawings have all been made by Mr. Wainwright and the photographs by a native Arab workman.

Since 1915 Mr. Wainwright has been in Egypt and I in Russia; the account of the excavations at Sawama therefore still remains to be written, but we hope that it may be published during the coming year. In the meantime, those interested may consult our preliminary report in the *Journal of Egyptian Archaeology*, vol. i, pp. 246–7.

All the objects from Balabish, except those reserved for the Cairo Museum, are in America. Their present location is indicated in each case in the Appendix to this volume.

CONTENTS.

LIST OF ABBREVIATIONS

USED IN QUOTING WORKS OF REFERENCE IN THE FOOTNOTES.

A.S.N. . . .	The *Archaeological Survey of Nubia*. *Reports* for 1907 to 1910 and *Bulletin* covering the same period, by Reisner, Firth and others.
Ä.Z. . . .	*Zeitschrift für ägyptische Sprache*.
B., *A.R.*	Breasted, Ancient Records.
L.A.A.A.	Annals of Archaeology and Anthropology, issued by the Institute of Archaeology, University of Liverpool.
Lacau, *Sarcophages*	Lacau, *Sarcophages antérieurs au Nouvel Empire* (*Catalogue Général du Musée du Caire*).
L., *D.*	Lepsius, *Denkmäler aas Ägypten und Äthiopen*.
N., *B.H.*	Newberry, *Beni Hasan*.
P., *C.A.*	Peet, *Cemeteries of Abydos*.
P., *D.P.*	Petrie, *Diospolis Parva*.
P., *G.R.*	Petrie, *Gizeh and Rifeh*.
P., *H.I.C.*	Petrie, *Hyksos and Israelite Cities*.
P., *I.K.G.*	Petrie, *Illahun, Kahun and Gurob*.
P., *K.G.H.*	Petrie, *Kahun, Gurob and Hawara*.
P., *L.G.M.*	Petrie and others, *The Labyrinth, Gerzeh and Mazghuneh*.
P., *N.B.*	Petrie, *Naqada and Ballas*.
P., *R.T.*	Petrie, *Royal Tombs of the Earliest Dynasties*.
S., *Pyr.*	Sethe, *Die Altaegyptischen Pyramidentexte*.
S., *Urk.*	Sethe, *Urkunden der 18. Dynastic*.

BALABISH

CHAPTER I.

THE SITE, BURIALS, DATING EVIDENCE, &c.

Plates I, XV.

THE SITE.

THE site selected for this season's work on behalf
of the American Branch of the Egypt Exploration
Society was at Balabish on the eastern bank of
the Nile, just at the upper end of the triangular
piece of land enclosed between the river and the
eastern desert. At our village, however, the
Nile still hugs the cliff and runs within three
quarters of an hour's walk of the desert edge.
Though a long way by river, Balabish is actually
only a little E.S.E. of Baliana, for between the
two the Nile takes a sharp double curve, and for
a short distance flows W.S.W. The site is
situated about equally distant from the railway
stations of Baliana or Abu Tisht, perhaps slightly
farther from the former than from the latter.
As may easily be imagined, it is a district very
much cut off from the rest of the world.
Balabish is a small village not shown on
Baedeker's map, but corresponding in position
to that called Gababish in the *Description de
l'Égypte*.[1] The name does not sound Arabic
and may come down from ancient days, as without doubt does that of Samhoud just opposite.
Moreover, it is situated in a neighbourhood
which was important from the earliest times

---

[1] See *Atlas*, Flle. 10.

while, someone at Baliana being thirsty had
drunk from the Nile and found it sweet, which
raised the alarm, and so the thieves were tracked
by the very means which they had hoped would
cover up their crime. Anyone who has had
dealings with them could quite believe the story
true. Indeed, the whole of this triangular area
and the narrow strip adjoining it, forming a sort
of *cul-de-sac* squeezed in between the Nile and
the desert, is an out-of-the-way place, and is
noted for the stupidity of its population. A
tale is told against the inhabitants of Awlad
Yahia, at the bottom end of this district, which
makes them out to be nearly as foolish as their
neighbours of Balabish. The story goes that
they, admiring one of the minarets of the
famous mosque of Girga, came into town one
night, put ropes round it, and proposed to draw
it away to their own village, but naturally they
were unsuccessful. The name given to another
apparently ancient site in this neighbourhood,
Kôm-el-magânîn, "Mound of the lunatics," just
opposite Balabish, rounds off the unenviable
reputation of the district.

The cemeteries of Balabish are situated just
behind the southernmost of the Balabish villages,
and lie on a triangular ridge in a vast torrent-
bed. This is quite clear in the central view on
Pl. I. The photographs are taken from the
centre of the triangular ridge, and beyond its
edge, especially in the central photograph, can
be seen the great southern part of the low-
lying torrent-bed stretching away to the next
ridge, about level with the point of the arrow,
which makes its southern bank. The points of
the spurs forming the base of the great triangular
ridge towards the cultivation are occupied by the
pan-grave cemetery. One is shown in the
photograph, and there are two smaller ones
similarly situated on the other two points next
to the north. They are not included here, as
there was a long stretch of virgin desert between
them; it was not easy to fit them in in an
intelligible manner, and nothing was to be learnt

pan-graves, we presume there must be a cemetery of that date in the neighbourhood whence the pot was borrowed. So far we have been unable to find it, and think it likely to be buried beneath the Nile mud which has encroached considerably on the desert.

TYPES OF TOMB.

There was no sign whatever of any brickwork, superstructure, or mound over the pan-graves, the desert surface being quite hard and smooth. The great majority of the pan-graves were either round or oval pits, about five feet in depth. In this they differ entirely from the shallow graves found by Prof. Petrie at Hu,[1] whence he named them "pan-graves," but are similar to those which he excavated at Rifeh very much farther to the north, not far from Assiut. However, these cemeteries clearly all belong to the same class, so many and important are the similarities between the civilizations of the three sites, though each naturally presents some details in which it varies from the others. Thus we are able to take them as a whole.

There were three types of graves :—

1. Cylindrical pits of a very accurately circular section with contracted burials. Type 1, Pl. XV, and Catalogue Pl. XVI.

2. Oval pits also with contracted burials. Type 2, Pl. XV, and Catalogue Pl. XVI.

3. Long graves with extended burials. Types 3, 4, Pl. XV, and Catalogue Pl. XVII.

To which may be added :—

4. Deposits of objects in small irregular holes without burials. Catalogue Pl. XVII.

The graves of whatever type were practically all cut in the hard gravel of the desert, but B 214, 223, were cut down into the underlying marl. One of the circular graves, B 181, expanded below, making a section like that of a wide-necked bottle. Of the oval pits· three,

THE BURIALS.

---

[1] These are similar to the latest C-group graves in Nubia, cf. *A.S.N.*, 1909–10, pp. 16, 138 ff.

equal, as in type 2, Plate XV. This was the case in nos. B 223, 224.

In the long graves the body was or had been extended, and strangely enough was twice lying on its face, in B 201, 238. Although it is possible that this was the work of plunderers in the case of B 201, the burial of B 238 was intact, with an unbroken coating of henna (?) paste about 1 cm. thick over the whole. Therefore this must have been the original position.

No. B 231 was lying on the back with hands on the pelvis. In every case in which anything like order remained, i.e. in B 184, 201, 231, 238, the head was regularly at the north end of the grave and the feet at the south.

The graves were oriented north or north-west very regularly, only B 220, 224 turning to the east of north. Thus the graves were no doubt following the course of the Nile, and were intended to be turned to the *local* north, which seems to have been judged by the direction of the river. Orientation to the north was adopted by the latest C-group people of Nubia, and began to appear in the earlier period.[1]

Whether the body had originally been made into a bundle and tied up in a skin we could not decide. There were generally remains of leather in the graves and often a great quantity. Scraps of leather cord also remained, hence the leather was no doubt tied up in a bundle. But whether this was just a bundle of leather, as in B 235 (Pl. XI, 2), where some cord still remains in place round it, or whether the body was tied up in a leather bundle, as is suggested by the bit of cord which remained on the leather covering at the neck of B 224, was not apparent. It is quite likely that it was customary to tie the bodies up in a bundle, for we understand this was done by the C-group people at Faras in Nubia, to whom our pan-grave people are related. It was also done in the proto-dynastic age, to which the

. . .

---

[1] *A.S.N.*, 1909–10, p. 13.

[2] PETRIE, *Tarkhan*, i, Pl. xxvi.

Mats had been used in B 181, 235, 238, 239. They were of two types :—

1. That found in B 181, 235 was made by arranging the reeds alongside of each other and piercing them through with others at some distance from each other. (Fig. 1.)

Fig. 1.

2. The type found in B 238, 239, in which the cross-pieces were again some distance apart but were arranged in pairs. The reeds forming the warp pass over and under, crossing each other between the members of each pair. (Fig. 2.) Probably each pair was fastened at the ends to keep it from splaying apart, but we found none showing the edges.[1]

Fig. 2.

EVIDENCE FOR DATE.

The pan-grave people are known from only a very few sites, and these are strictly confined to southern Egypt. The most northerly of their settlements hitherto discovered is at Rifeh, just south of Assiut. The other sites are Balabish about opposite Abydos, Diospolis Parva a little farther to the south, Deir el Ballas[2] opposite Quft (Koptos), and el Khizam[2] again a little farther south, and just north of Thebes.

In his original survey of the newly discovered pan-grave civilization Prof. Petrie assigned it to the Intermediate Period between the Middle and New Kingdoms.[3] At Balabish we found plenty of evidence corroborating his conclusion. A quantity of objects were found of Middle Kingdom or Intermediate style, such as blue marble *kohl*-pots, axes, red rimmed and red painted *situla* vases. We did not find any of the pre-XIIth Dynasty button-seals, such as are

---

[1] A fine example of this type of mat is photographed and published in P., *G.R.*, Pl. x, F.

[2] REISNER, *A.S.N. Bulletin*, no. 4, p. 12.　Reprinted *A.S.N.*, 1908-09, p. 18.

[3] P., *D.P.*, p. 48.

[4] *A.S.N.*, 1907-08, Pl. 71, a, b, nos. 14-16, 36. Cf. p. 335. *A.S.N.*, 1908-09, Pl. 52, b, nos. 30-34.

from the black spheroid beads, and this, though
negative, suggests that the pan-graves ceased
about the beginning of the XVIIIth Dynasty.
Black spheroids were common both in the pan-
graves and in the New Kingdom cemetery. But
when we examined them closely we found that,
though the majority of these New Kingdom
beads were of black semi-transparent glass, *no
single glass bead was discoverable in a pan-grave.
The pan-grave black spheroids were invariably
of glaze.* The absence of glass was similarly
striking in the case of the penannular earrings.
Though glass was used for some of the small ones
from the New Kingdom graves, this material
was not used for the pan-grave specimens, which
were of shell. The small one from B 220
(Pl. VII, 2) much resembled opaque white glass
until examined closely, when its true nature was
apparent. This absence of glass is fairly strong
evidence that the pan-grave civilization had
ceased before the use of glass for beads and
ornaments had become common. As stated
above, this had taken place by the latter half
of the New Kingdom, and the use of transparent glass for beads is contemporary with the
beginning of the XVIIIth Dynasty, for there is
a large ball bead of this substance in the Ashmolean Museum bearing the name of Zeser-ka-ra
(Amenhotep I), the second king of this dynasty.

Corroborative evidence that the pan-graves did
not last on into the XVIIIth Dynasty is forthcoming from a study of the life history of the
disc beads. As shown on p. 22, the white disc
beads of ostrich-egg shell are very common in
almost all ages of Egyptian civilization until the
XVIIIth Dynasty, when they suddenly cease,
and in their place we find great quantities of
small disc beads of red, yellow or blue glaze.
As the egg-shell discs are very characteristic of
the pan-graves, it is evident that the civilization belongs to the pre-XVIIIth Dynasty group,
and it is improbable that it runs on into the
age that discarded these beads. Further, the
XVIIIth Dynasty red, blue and yellow glaze

---

[1] P., *G.R.*, pp. 20, 21.

[2] See Petrie's conclusions, *G.R.*, pp. 20, 21.

[3] We found three axes, bow-strings, three bracers or
archers' wrist-guards, and arrows were found at Rifeh ; and
the Mazoi of Lower Nubia, from which country the pan-
grave people also came, were drawn on for soldiery to assist
in expelling the Hyksos (GRIFFITH in CARNARVON, *Five
Years Exploration at Thebes*, p. 37).

to all intents and purposes becomes absorbed by the *fellâhîn.* We know nothing about these kings except that they arose in the South, presumably at Thebes, in the neighbourhood of the site of the large pan-grave cemetery of El Khizam.[1] However, Prof. Petrie sees a facial resemblance between them and the Barabra, and hence suggests that they came from Ethiopia.[2] They became the saviours of Egypt by casting out the Semitic Hyksos, and they incidentally built up a kingdom for themselves. This, then, would not be so dissimilar from the course of events under Piankhy and Tirhakah, where we know that warlike Nubians possessed of initiative set up as orthodox Egyptian Pharaohs, uniting the Two Lands in the case of Piankhy, or opposing the newest Semitic invaders, the Assyrians, in the case of Tirhakah.

There is, however, another Nubian tribe who might claim to be the progenitors of the royal line. This is the people of the black-topped cups with the flared rims and grey bands whom we discover in Egypt in the XVIIth Dynasty.[3] These people no doubt come from Kerma in the Dongola Province, and seem to be connected with the XVIIth or early XVIIIth Dynasties in their use of the large fly ornaments so well known under Ahmose.[4] Unfortunately we are still in the dark as to the sequences and details of the Kerma archaeology, which must form the foundation of any true view of this race; but, apart from the uncertainty induced by our present ignorance of the Kerma evidence, such indications as there are seem to point to the belief that those men were not the founders of the XVIIth Dynasty, but rather the Ethiopians whose advances gave so much trouble in the early part of the New Kingdom.

---

[1] *A.S.N. Bull.,* no. 4, p. 12, reprinted *A.S.N.,* 1908–9, p. 18.

[2] PETRIE, *History of Egypt,* ii, p. 4.

[3] See further p. 52.

[4] MacIVER and WOOLLEY, *Buhen,* Pl. 51; REISNER, *Ä.Z.,* 1914, Taf. iv; BISSING, *Thebanischer Grabfund,* vi, 2, 3, a.b.

[5] GRIFFITH in CARNARVON, *Five Years Exploration at Thebes,* p. 36.

[6] B., *A.R.,* ii, § 7; PETRIE, *History,* ii, pp. 5–7.

[7] B., *A.R.,* ii, 15; SETHE, *Urk.,* iv, 5.

[8] Kamose and Ahmose are figured at Toshkeh (WEIGALL, *Antiquities of Lower Nubia,* Pl. lxv, 4), north of the Second Cataract. Amenhotep I, their successor, reached a little farther to the south, but is not known beyond Uronarti, just south of the Second Cataract (B., *A.R.,* ii, § 38), while his successor Tuthmosis I set up an inscription and built a fortress on the Island of Tombos just above the Third Cataract (B., *A.R.,* ii, 67, 72).

CHAPTER II.

TOMB GROUPS (PAN-GRAVES).

Plates II, III, IV, VI and VII.

PLATE II, NO. 1. TOMB GROUP B 110.

THE saucer is of the ordinary New Kingdom type of rough brown pottery. It has been rubbed down to its present size from a larger vessel, as an inspection of the edge shows. A small hole has also been knocked in the bottom. The beads of the first string are of types 2, 17, 18, 19' in the second of types 1, 1 B, and in the third mostly of type 3. There were a great number of shells. Those shown in the Plate are mostly *Nerita sc. polita* (type 2). For a full list of the types represented see the Catalogue of Graves on Pl. XVI. In the lowest row on the left are two small palettes of stone with a pink pebble rubber; in the centre is a curious stone notched at one end, which has a few longitudinal scratches on it, but no clear sign of having been used as a palette; next is a black-topped potsherd which had been rubbed down into an oval shape to serve as a digger or scraper (?); and lastly, a very thin plate of copper or bronze of undetermined use. This last seems too thin to serve any practical use, and hence would appear to be a personal ornament, though it is not pierced for suspension.

PLATE II, NO. 2. TOMB GROUP B 208.

A very fine group, coming from a full-sized long and deep rectangular grave, which had been utterly plundered. For plan see Pl. XV, no. 3. All these objects were found in a pile against the eastern wall of the grave. On disturbing the sand a very strong scent of ointment, similar to that of the pre- and proto-dynastic age, was observed, though none of the pots contained any of the material.

The pottery types accompanying the objects will be found on Pl. XIV, H 5, Buff 2, 3, 7, Borrowed 2, 4, 5, 10. It is a curiously mixed lot, in that it includes a true pre-dynastic pot of type D 5 b and the little saucers or covers Borrowed 4, 5, 10, which might belong to any age. No. 5 especially gives evidence of its secondhand origin in being nothing but the base of an old pot, which has been rubbed down round the edges to accommodate it to its new use as a cover to a jar of type Buff 7. It has also been notched on the edge. For comparison with the cover no. 10 the reader should refer to *The Labyrinth, Gerzeh and Mazghuneh*, Pl. xviii, 55. No. 4 is made of the ordinary brown pottery of the New Kingdom and is blackened inside. There is nothing to notice individually in the representatives of the Buff ware from this group, therefore they will be treated with the rest of their type. A good example of type Buff 7 will be found photographed on Pl. V, 1. The pre-dynastic pot is of the clay usual to the pots of this D class, but has turned an exceptionally yellow-green colour owing to its having been over-fired. This colour, though unusual, is found from time to time in the D pottery of the pre-dynastic civilization. The presence of this pot in a pan-grave should be compared with that of the pre-dynastic potsherds, evidently also of type D (no. 67c probably *Naqada and Ballas*, Pl. xxxv), which were found in grave 72 : 218

of the Nubian C-group.[1] In neither case was there a pre-dynastic cemetery near from which these pots could have been accidentally transferred by plunderers. Twice again pots of pre-dynastic type are recorded in C-group graves,[2] and yet another has been found by the Oxford Expedition to Nubia in the C-group cemetery at Faras, which will be published shortly. The bowl H 5, which is photographed in our group, was a very fine specimen of its class, and the only perfect example which we found. The other side of it will be found in Pl. V, 2. The *kohl*-pot is of blue marble, a substance characteristic of the Middle Kingdom, but not unknown in the early New Kingdom, in which horizon we found it at Sawamah.[3] This specimen belongs to the most common of the pan-grave types of *kohl*-pot, no. 13 (Pl. XIII), though the workmanship of the neck differs from that of the drawn specimen and approximates to that of type 14. For the shells see further, p. 18. Here it need only be mentioned that they are *Cypraea* (?) *pantherina*, type 17 ; *Malea pomum* (probably), type 18 ; *Strombus*, sp. uncertain, type 19 ; and *Charonia tritonis*, type 20 ; besides which there is a smallish shell of the *Conus* species with a hole in the end of it, shown in the plate near the piece of webbing. This latter is perhaps a belt. Beside the small shell are two small black pebbles, and on the lower row are three bone awls or borers.

PLATE III, NO. 1. TOMB GROUP B 185.

The only example we found of a prepared ox-skull. With it was the ram's horn. There were no other objects in the grave except relics of a male skeleton, as the whole had been plundered

---

[1] *A.S.N.*, 1908–9, p. 83.

[2] *A.S.N.*, 1908–9, p. 160, no. 14 ; *A.S.N.*, 1909–10, p. 132, no. 360.

[3] See also GARSTANG, *El Arabah*, p. 29 ; CURRELLY, *Abydos*, iii, Pl. lix, 5, 6.

[4] P., *D.P.*, p. 48.

[5] P., *G.R.*, for a cemetery in this neighbourhood.

PLATE III, NO. 2. TOMB GROUP B 201.

From a long grave. No. 1 is a curious horn
object of concavo-convex section, as is shown on
Pl. XII, 6 (see further, p. 31). Next to it are
several scraps of fine leather, dyed red, with
little blue beads of type 3 stitched on. No. 2
is a delicate tortoise-shell bracelet of flat section,
for which see Pl. XX, 10. This delicate flat
section seems to occur in the C-group tortoise-
shell bracelets (?) from Nubia.[1] But here the
resemblance ceases, as these latter are penannular
in form, whereas ours is a ring cut out of the
solid piece. No. 5 is a penannular object of horn
of flat section, shown as no. 5, Pl. XII. No. 6 is
a curved horn object of concavo-convex section (a
strigil?), shown as no. 8, Pl. XII. It is no doubt
the remains of another specimen of this type.
No. 7 is a copper casting of the forepart of a
kneeling ram (see better Pl. XIII, 3), the hinder
part being merely a bar of square section. It is
a secondhand object, as the bar projecting from
behind is broken off short.

The axe, no. 8, was still fixed into a slot in the
remains of its wooden handle, but there were no
signs of binding. having been used, such as
remained on the other axe-head from B 226,
Pl. VI, no. 1, and on the similar Ahmose axe.
Perhaps it had been fastened by two collars
slipping over the projecting ends, as was so often
the case.[2] No. 9, the *kohl*-pot, is a variety of
type 14 (Pl. XIII). It is made of alabaster, and
has been provided with a lid roughly modelled
in pottery, and too small for it. This custom of
providing a new lid to a *kohl*-pot was observed
in the New Kingdom grave B 34, where an
alabaster *kohl*-pot had been provided with a
black serpentine lid which was too small for it.
No. 10 is the string of carnelian barrel beads
which figures again in Pl. VIII as string no. 12.
The single melon bead at the end shows up well
again here. These beads come from the neck.

,,

---

[1] *A.S.N.*, 1908–9, Pl. 37c, 9.
[2] P., *D.P.*, xxxii, 21.

[3] For full discussion see Chap. V.

PLATE IV, no. 1. TOMB GROUP B 212.

From a circular grave utterly plundered, with
no bones left. In the filling were found the
small saucer of *qulleh* ware with a hole pierced
in the bottom, an oval potsherd used as a digger
or scraper, and the small footed bowl, which was
painted red. There were also four pieces of
white material, presumably shell, of which two
pieces appear on the right-hand side of the
photograph. They were very much perished,
and to-day resemble nothing so much as the
cuttle-fish bone given to canaries. Below are
several flint flakes, the only ones found in the
pan-graves. Below these again are pieces of
spongy metallic-looking haematite. There is
also a piece of stone which the authorities of the
South Kensington Natural History Museum find
on examination to be sandstone stained green
with copper. It may have served as a cheap
substitute for malachite. On the extreme right
will be seen a piece of red haematite, which has
been much rubbed down on all sides for use
as a pigment. Samples of the haematite as
well as of the malachite were submitted to the
authorities of the South Kensington Museum,
who vouch for the materials. To the uninitiated
observer the spongy haematite looks much like
the dross or scoriae from a smelting furnace
which still contains a large percentage of metal.
In the middle are two awls, one of bone, the
other of copper or bronze, hafted in a small
wooden handle now much decayed. There was
another similar implement, of bone and broken.
It is represented among the spatulae or hair-pins
of Pl. VII, no. 4. The awls are probably for
boring leather, since implements similar to the
copper one are being used for this purpose in
the scenes from the tomb of Rekhmire.[1] A
number of the shells found are figured, also the
beads. Those in the short strings in the upper
row consist of type 3, those in the middle row
are of type 1, while the lowest row of all is a

string of similar shell disc beads, but in an
unfinished state. This figures among the types
in Pl. VIII as string no. 18. In the same plate,
no. 2, is a group of these unfinished beads which
have not yet even been bored.

"

---

[1] NEWBERRY, *The Life of Rekhmara*, Pl. xviii.

[2] DUFTON, *A Journey through Abyssinia*, 1867, p. 98.

[3] VEITCH, *Views in Central Abyssinia*, 1868, no. 38.

[4] JEAN DUCHESNE-FOURNET, *Mission en Éthiopie*, 1901–3
ii, p. 295.

[5] SETHE, *Urk.*, iv, 84 = B., *A.R.*, ii, 71 ; SETHE, *op. cit.*
iv, 613 = B., *A.R.*, ii, 657, and the correction v, p. vii.

[6] SELIGMANN, *Some Aspects of the Hamitic Problem*,
Journ. Roy. Anthrop. Instit., xliii, p. 618, and BRUGSCH,
Dict., ⌒ ⌣ *nbd.*

it may be better translated "with braided or plaited hair." The Libyan sidelock may be connected with this. It is sometimes plaited and not merely twisted.[1] If Lepsius is accurate in this detail, it would be significant that some Libyans are shown[2] with hair in ridges (plaits?) running from the forehead back over the head, just as King Theodore's hair is described. The Egyptian lock of youth is often shown as plaited.[3] Thus the presence of short locks of hair in this grave is no criterion of sex. The pierced leather was found near the pelvis, as was the similar material in B 184. The presumption, therefore, is that it was in both cases the remains of a kilt. With it was found the charming little bag of woven elephants' (?) hair. A cup of black-topped ware, type B 2, and also a piece of a bowl of red polished ware, type Borrowed 1, were found, as was the piece of curved horn, no. 9 on Pl. XII. Other objects found here were pebbles, small blue beads, and pieces of leather. Attention should also be called to several large black feathers, possibly the wing or tail feathers of a crow or some such bird. We had supposed that they had been introduced by accident while the grave was open at the time of the plundering, but we find they also occurred in three C-group graves in Nubia,[4] all of which, like the present tomb, contained male bodies. Mr. Griffith tells us he has also found feathers, though apparently of a different sort, in C-group graves at Faras in Nubia. There would, therefore, seem to have been a custom among this people of burying feathers especially with men. In the second of the Nubian graves quoted, pierced leather was also found with the feathers as here. This grave belongs to cemetery no. 58, of mixed C-group and New Kingdom graves, and though this grave, no. 121, is classed as of the latter date, there seems nothing to prevent its being an extended C-group burial.

---

[1] BATES, *The Eastern Libyans*, p. 135.

[2] *Denkmäler*, iii, 136a.

[3] For instance, PRISSE, *Histoire de l'Art Ég.*: Portrait de Ramsès-Meiamoun, &c.

[4] *A.S.N.*, 1908–9, p. 58, no. 108, where they are stated to have been black, p. 60, no. 121, p. 64, no. 1.

case the ankle-straps have been bound with leather, though the binding has disappeared, except for a small fragment on the left sandal. (See further, p. 25.) Between the sandals are the beads, consisting of types 1, 12, 13, white disc beads and spheroids of carnelian and green felspar. Besides these there is a curved horn object, pointed at each end, and of a concavo-convex section, of which we found several (see Pl. XII, 8). We can only suggest that it might be a species of strigil. This instrument was used in antiquity by the Greeks and Romans, and to-day the Kaffirs scrape off the sweat with a sharp-edged bone implement, though not of this shape, but more like the blunt-pointed bone objects on Pl. VII, fig. 4. Perhaps our examples may be ancient representatives of the "thin curved skewer, of hard wood or ibex horn, thrust through his hair," which the desert Hamite, north of Port Sudan, wears to-day;[1] but it is impossible to be certain, as no further details are given. An iron strigil of the classical shape, but probably of XXVIth Dynasty date, was found at Tell el-Yahudiyeh.[2]

PLATE VII, NO. 1. TOMB GROUP B 220.

From a circular grave with a male skeleton. A black-topped bowl of red polished ware, type B 2, see also Pl. V, no. 2. A number of calcite crystals, among which will be found one of the several shells of type 2 which we found. A tiny penannular earring of shell. Another, also of shell but much thicker, was found in grave B 236. White shell disc beads type no. 1. There were also a few of the tiny blue beads type 3.

PLATE VII, NO. 2. TOMB GROUP B 239.

From the filling of a circular grave. A rounded potsherd of *qulleh* ware used perhaps as a scraper or digger. A piece of leather wrapped on to a piece of wood of semicircular section,

PLATE VII, NO. 3. TOMB GROUP B 182.

From a small irregular hole in the ground roughly triangular in shape and without any

---

[1] C. CROSSLAND, *Desert and Water Gardens of the Red Sea*, p. 24. [2] P., *H.I.C.*, Pl. xxi, 8, and p. 19.

[3] Cf. the C-group cordage reported *A.S.N.*, 1907-8, p. 54, no. 174.

signs of a burial. The curved horn object is another of the strigil-like implements, highly decorated with incised patterns, as will be seen from the drawing on Pl. XII, no. 7. It has been bored with two comparatively large holes near the end, each about a quarter of an inch in diameter. It was originally longer and had been mended with a copper strip, but the broken part has again been broken off and has now disappeared. It came from the south end of the hole, and near it lay the horn bracelet (see also Pl. XII, no. 5, and p. 31), made of a plain horn bent round until the tip and butt met. The few beads were white discs of type 1 and had once been sewn into leather. In the centre of the hole was a pot of Buff ware, type 9 (Pl. XIV), full of ointment scented like that of the pre- and proto-dynastic age, and wrapped up in woven material. The pot is exceptionally green in colour and is now very much stained with the ointment. The presence of the beads which had once been sewn into leather suggests the possibility of this deposit representing a plundered burial; but this seems hardly possible owing to the smallness and shallowness of the hole, which completely differentiate it from any of the the graves. Moreover, the pot was standing upright in the centre of the hole and occupying most of the room, and it can hardly be a chance that the only other hole of a similar nature, B 223, also contained a large pot of the same ware, type 7 (Pl. XIV), also full of the same ointment. This pot was sealed, and nothing else was found with it.

The ointment is entirely similar to that found in the pre- and proto-dynastic period, as at Naqada and Ballas and Tarkhan. In the New Kingdom cemetery at Balabish the same scent emanated from a black polished jug no. B 66 and a false-necked amphora no. B 87. When found the ointment is a beautiful clean yellow of the colour of butter and of a crumbly consistency. If exposed to the hot Egyptian sun it will melt. On such occasions it exudes a dark brown treacly

[1] See P., *N.B.*, pp. 11, 39.

[2] PLINY, xii, 25 (54) says that balsamum "has been only bestowed by nature upon the land of Judea. In former times it was cultivated in two gardens only."

STRABO, *C* 763, speaks of Jericho as being "encompassed by a mountainous district which slopes towards it somewhat in the manner of a theatre. . . . Here also is a palace and the garden of the balsamum."

DIODORUS SICULUS, ii, 48, says that near the Dead Sea

likely, as it is only mentioned in the Old
Testament in the Song of Solomon, which is
of· post-exilic date, though well known in the
New Testament[1] and in classical times. The
knowledge of it seems to have come from
India,[2] and the Hebrew name *nĕrd* is said to be
derived from Sanskrit.[3] Hence it probably was

---

balsamum is produced in a certain hollow, and that it
grows nowhere else.

THEOPHRASTUS, *Hist. Plant.*, ix, 6, says "balsamum is
produced in the hollow about Syria."

JUSTIN, xxxvi, 3, says that "opobalsamum is produced
only in that country (Judea); for there is.a valley which
is shut in by continuous mountains as if by a wall in the
likeness of gardens (camp in other editions), the space
enclosed being about two hundred *jugera*, and called by the
name of Ericus (or Hierichus, Jericho)." He then describes
the· opobalsamum trees, and speaks of the warmth of the
sun in this valley, and remarks that the sun in that climate
is the hottest in the world.

Now Schweinfurth has shown that the balsam of the
ancients was, not as has generally been supposed Balm of
Gilead, but most probably what is now known as Mecca
balsam, produced by the *Balsamodendron opobalsamum*, a
tropical tree widely distributed over the coast territory of
Arabia, the adjacent isles, and S. Nubia (*Pharm. Journal*,
April, 1894, p. 897). This has caused doubt to be cast on
the classical statements that the tree grew in a country so
far north as Judea, but it really confirms them. For the
more detailed statements show that the part of Syria or
Judea where it grew was a hollow near Jericho, evidently
the deep Jordan Valley. Justin, who gives us the most
complete account, describes the place as shut in by continuous mountains like a wall, which is a peculiarity of
this valley. His reference to the extreme heat of
the sun in the valley is also of importance, as the
tropical heat of the Jordan Valley is well known to-
day. In May a noon-day temperature of 105° has been
registered; hence the land bears a "strange sub-tropical
vegetation" quite out of keeping with its latitude (ELLIS-
WORTH PARTINGTON, *Palestine and its Transformation*,
pp. 201, 229). Thus what is known to ·be only a tropical
plant would have flourished only at the particular spot
in Palestine to which it is so continuously referred by
the classical writers. JOSEPHUS, viii, 6, 6, moreover, says
definitely that it was transplanted from the districts in
which it is now widely distributed, for he says, "we possess
the root of that opobalsamum which our country still bears
by this woman's (the Queen of Sheba) gift."

[1] Cf. John iii. 3.

[2] Cf. PLINY, xiii, 1 (2).

[3] BROWN, DRIVER and BRIGGS, *Hebrew Lexicon*, p. 660.

[4] PLINY, *Nat. Hist.*, xii, 12 (26).

[5] BROWN, DRIVER and BRIGGS, *Hebrew Lexicon*, p. 141,
gives the references.

[6] PLINY, *Nat. Hist.*, xii, 25 (54); JOSEPHUS, *Antiqq. of
the Jews*, xiv, 481; *The Jewish War*, i, 6, 6.

TOMB GROUP B 181 (see Pl. XV, 1).

The tomb consisted of a cylindrical pit of diameter 0·95 m., and depth 1·65 m., cut in the gravel, and opening out a little below.

The body was contracted, lying on its right side with the head at 340° and faced west. Much skin remained, and the body was *covered* with a thick layer of woven material, over which was spread a mat of the pierced type. Under the head lay 9, perhaps as a pillow.

1. Pot of hard thick pinkish ware. Type Buff 8.

2. Black-topped bowl. Type B 6.

3. Strings of small blue beads at r. ankle. Type 3.

CHAPTER III.

SHELLS, AMULETS, BEADS, &c.

Plates VII, VIII, XIII.

OBJECTS OF BONE.

SHELLS.

Plate VII, 4. Examples of bone spatulae or hair-pins (?) and bone borers. No. B 180 and that without a number àre made from the *tibiae* of sheep, hence probably the others are also. These hair-pins are of a flat oval section, with blunt edges and points. Thus they are not unlike the strigils used to-day by the Kaffirs of South Africa and kept in the hair. That the pre-dynastic people were accustomed to keep sundry toilet objects in their hair is shown by the photograph B 378, P., *D.P.* Pl. vi. Only three of these spatulae were found, all of which come from circular or oval graves. Borers, like spatulae, were uncommon. They were found with other objects only in graves B 208, 212 ; cf. Pls. II, 2, IV, 1. The specially fine example shown in . this plate was unfortunately an isolated object. Pointed bones, similar to those of B 208, were found in the Aahmes town at Abydos,[1] and would therefore be a little later in date than these. They are described as netting bones. None of ours had an eyelet-hole, as had an undated specimen from the Osiris Temple at Abydos.[2] Pointed bones are very rare in the pre-dynastic age,[3] as also is the use of leather, so it is possible that the one necessitated the other, and that these bone awls are for boring leather preparatory to receiving the stitches.

Plate VIII, 2. One of the great characteristics of the pan-graves at Balabish was the profusion of shells which came to light. Altogether twenty different species were represented. A type set is published on this plate, to which must be added the large examples on Pl. II, 2. The list of names, kindly supplied by the experts of the South Kensington Natural History Museum, is appended here. Types 17, 18, 19, 20, went straight to America, therefore it was only possible to submit the photograph for identi cation :—

---

[1] *Abydos*, iii, Pl. lvii.
[2] *Abydos*, i, Pl. li.
[3] For the only specimens we know, see GARSTANG, *El Mahásna and Bét Khalláf*, Pl. iv.

Nos. 1, 11, are modern Nile species, and with the exception of no. 13, the rest are not Mediterranean but Red Sea or Indian Ocean forms. There is some doubt about the true locality of no. 13.

Of these types by far the most common was no. 2, both as regards the number of graves in which it appeared, and also the numbers by which it was represented. The large open shell, which was in such continual request in Egypt, was found here in the Nile species *Spatha* (?) *rubens*, type 1. The little *Pusiostoma mendicaria*, type 12, one has seen imitated in paste. Similarly a small *Conus*, such as type 9, is copied in jasper in the XIIth Dynasty,[1] and the Ashmolean Museum possesses a string of such shells in blue frit, also of this date. The carnelian and felspar shell beads of the XIIth Dynasty, recorded in *Riqqeh*, Pl. xli, 146, are also copies of small *Conus* shells (see Bead Cases of Edwards' Library). Many of the shells were bored for suspension, and in B 207 we found fragments of the leather thread on which they had been strung still remaining in place. But besides those which had been bored, there were many which had not been so treated. It would be supposed that these were stock in hand against the time when they should be required. But there was evidently a fondness for shells for their own sake, as is evidenced by the beautiful specimens from B 208 (Pl. II, 2). While the big *Triton* has had a hole pierced in it the other three have not been worked, but are in a state of nature. It would therefore seem that they had been treasured as valuable or sacred objects, and not as personal ornaments. The same might apply to the *Triton* shell, which is so large that it could hardly have been worn on the person. Was it hung up as a charm about the house or elsewhere by means of its suspension hole? Large shells, though of a different species from any of those here repre-

sented, had been sacred objects at a much earlier time, for two are sculptured on each of the three proto-dynastic Min statues from Koptos.[2]

From the same period comes the necklace of golden imitation shells.[3] Large flat mother-of-pearl shells of a discoid shape are not uncommon in Egypt. They often bear the name of Senusert, inscribed in the middle.[4] As they are often bored at the point, they were, no doubt, used as pectorals. Such a shell was occasionally copied in gold.[5] Shells of various species copied in gold formed an important part of the jewellery of the XIIth Dynasty,[6] and a large *Pinna* shell is reported as having been deposited with XIIth Dynasty pottery.[7]

A large shell was also found in the shaft-grave, with "Kerma-like," flared, black-topped cups,[8] and again in an XVIIIth Dynasty grave,[9] both at Abydos.

At Balabish we also found a string of white snail shells in the New Kingdom grave B 90.

On the whole subject of the use of shells, and the dating of the specimens, see the great mass of information published by Petrie.[10]

It is an interesting fact that no Mediterranean species is represented among these shells of ours. Though only natural for geographical reasons, yet it may one day prove of importance ethnologically. Except for the two Nile species, and the one doubtful species, they are all of Red Sea or Indian Ocean origin. A similar phenomenon

---

[1] PETRIE, *Dendereh*, Pl. xx, p. 22.

[2] PETRIE, *Koptos*, Pls. iii, iv, pp. 7, 8.

[3] R., *N.D.*, ii, Pl. 6, p. 139.

[4] See for instance PETRIE, *Amulets*, Pl. xliv, 112, a, Pl. xiv, 112, c, d, p. 27, no. 112, where others are quoted, and dated to the intermediate period between the XIIth and XVIIIth Dynasties.

[5] *Riqqeh*, Pl. i, 4.

[6] DE MORGAN, *Fouilles à Dahchour*, 1894, Pls. xvi, xvii, xxii, xxiii, xxiv, 1894–5, Pl. xii.

[7] ENGELBACH, *Riqqeh and Memphis VI*, p. 2.

[8] P., *C.A.*, ii, p. 62.

[9] P., *C.A.*, iii, Pl. xii, 6, p. 30, no. 17.

[10] *Amulets*, pp. 27, 28, Pls. xiv, xv, xliv.

was observed at the pre-dynastic site of El Amrah,[1] where the great majority of all the shells are of Red Sea origin. Eleven are from the Red Sea, possibly thirteen, while three come from the Nile, and only two are from the Mediterranean.

It is surprising that the cowrie-shell should be entirely absent from the twenty species discovered at Balabish, the more so as it was such a favourite with the C-group people in Nubia, and was much worn in later times in Egypt, as it is down to the present day. The whole genus *Cypraea* is only once represented, and that questionably, in the large *Cypraea pantherina*(?) of B 208.

AMULETS.

For a people who made so great a use of beads, the pan-grave people manufactured extraordinarily few amulets. In this they resemble the early pre-dynastic people. None are reported either in *Diospolis Parva* or in *Gizeh and Rifeh*, and in only one case, B 153, did we find a set, and then it only consisted of very few and of very inferior make. They are shown in photograph on Pl. VIII, 1, no. 16, and in outline Pl. XIII, nos. 7, 8, 9. In two other graves, B 183, 219 (Pl. XIII, 5, 6), we found single specimens, and except for the shells, which may also be amuletic, there were no others. They are all made of a poor quality glaze of a dark greenish-blue colour, and among them one notices the common fly, the Taurt figure, and a plain conical object, for which last see Pl. VIII. The other shapes are curious. On Pl. XIII there is no. 9 of thin section, which one can only imagine to be an axe-head of a type used in the XIIth Dynasty.[2] A number are known in our museums, and the Ashmolean possesses one from Dendereh, dated to the VIth Dynasty. Should

[1] MacIver and Mace, *El Amrah and Abydos*, p. 49.
[2] N., *B.H.*, i, Pl. xiv, &c. ; Garstang, *Burial Customs of Ancient Egypt*, fig. 165.

[3] P., *D.P.*, Pl. iv., p. 27.
[4] Petrie, *Abydos*, i, Pl. li, 2, 3, p. 23.
[5] P., *N.B.*, Pl. xlvii, 29 ; Ayrton, *Mahasna*, Pl. xv, 3.

D 2

noticeable that glass is entirely absent from the pan-grave material, and this makes a clearly defined cultural point. The commonest and at the same time the most distinctive classes of pan-grave beads are the white discs (type 1), and the tiny beads of bright blue glaze, which are very irregularly cut (type 3). Both these classes are sewn into the seams of leather to a large extent. Examples will be seen in Pls. X, XI of this use of the white and blue beads respectively, while on Pl. III, 2 will be seen another means of using them, by stitching them, not into the seams, but on to the surface of the leather, in this case a softly dressed leather of fine quality. However, they are also used in strings as in Pl. IV, 1. The habit of stitching beads into the seams of the leather is peculiar to the pan-grave people, and they admired the effect to such an extent that they introduced a double row instead of merely a single one (see Pl. X, 1). This seems to have been effected by the insertion of a piece of piping between the rows, as shown in section in fig. 3, but we were unable to make sure that the leather was not merely pierced with a double row of closely placed holes into which the beads were inserted and sewn. On the under side this process would have raised edges quite similar to those of a piping, and through these edges the thread passed. The leather would not bear very much handling as it was perished. The beads were strung either on leather threads as in Pl. X, 1, or on some fibrous material as in Pl. IV, 1.

Fig. 3.

In several cases we were able to observe how the beads were worn. The large carnelian barrel beads (Pl. VIII, no. 12) were round the neck, as were the blue disc beads in B 210. In B 231 a string of black spheroids was worn round the neck (Pl. VIII, no. 9). The burial richest in beads, B 181, had small blue beads on the right ankle, and on the left there was a double string of white disc and carnelian spheroid

[1] P., *L.G.M.*, p. 22.
[2] P., *D.P.*, p. 46.
[3] BATES, *The Eastern Libyans*, p. 132.

up in connection with the collection of examples on Pl. VIII. The term " spheroid" has been applied to all beads with rounded sides but flat ends, whether they are thick as in fig. 4, or thin as in fig. 5, since in either case the form is that of a section of a sphere. The thick ones thus approximate to the true ball bead, and the thinnest to the disc bead. The term "melon" refers to vertically furrowed spheroid beads, resembling a hot-house melon in shape. The term "collar" refers to short cylinders of wide diameter. They are made of very thin metal. They fit over the ends of the spheroid beads with which they are used, and thus correspond in metal to type 1A in shell, which has been hollowed to serve the same purpose. Similar, but much larger, gold collar beads, also used with hard stone spheroid beads (in these cases amethyst), were found in two tombs of the XIIth Dynasty at Wady Halfa.[1] Each type is described and is numbered for easy reference, and to each is added the numbers of the strings in Pl. VIII in which examples of that type will be found.

Disc beads.

Type 1. White discs, made almost certainly of ostrich egg shell. Strings nos. 5, 6, 11, 17. Unfinished specimens are numbered 2, 18 in the plate.

1A. White discs, hollowed out to take the spheroid beads. Strings 7, 8.

1B. Fish vertebrae used to supplement the white discs. Pl. II, 1.

2. Coarse blue glaze discs. String 5 in the centre.

3. Tiny brilliant blue glaze, very irregularly cut. String 15. No. 16 is similar, but of the dark greenish blue glaze. Pl. II, 1, third string, Pl. III, 3, third string.

4. Tiny black glaze, very irregularly cut. String 3.

---

[1] MacIver and Woolley, *Buhen,* Frontispiece to Text, and Pl. 87.

Drop beads.

    Type 25. Large fine light blue glaze. B 239.
        26. Small poor dark greenish blue glaze.
        String 16.

    The white disc beads would appear to be made of ostrich egg shell. A large number of unfinished ones were found (Pl. VIII, nos. 2, 18), some of which were submitted to the experts of the South Kensington Museum of Natural History, who report that they are " almost certainly ostrich egg shell." It is evident from the unfinished specimens that small pieces of shell were chipped to approximately the right size, then bored with a blunt point, and finally the rough edges were polished down. For this process they might have been tightly threaded on a string which would thus give a sufficient surface of edges on which to work. With these were occasionally found small fish vertebræ of suitable size. These being of a whitish colour served the purpose very well, and were no doubt easier to procure than the shell discs, which were only produced after a laborious rubbing down and boring. It is very noticeable that these white disc beads cease abruptly on the rise of the XVIIIth Dynasty, but begin to come in again during the XIXth, and are found in the XXIInd Dynasty. They had been very common throughout the earlier periods, i.e. in the pre-dynastic, apparently not in the Old Kingdom, in the Intermediate Period between the Old and Middle Kingdoms, in the Middle Kingdom, and in the pan-graves. In the XVIIIth Dynasty, when they drop out, their place is taken by the new brightly coloured discs of red, yellow and blue glaze. After the novelty of these has worn off they begin to come into fashion again.

    The ancient art of glazing crystal a blue colour was represented here in the large spheroid bead, type 5. It was the only example of this rare art which came to light. This probably constitutes another link with the pre- to proto-dynastic age, at which time this

[1] P., *N.B.*, pp. 44, 45; *Hierakonpolis*, ii, p. 39; PETRIE, *Abydos*, ii, p. 26, Pl. viii, nos. 171, 172, 174; see also Pls. vi, 63, vii, 84. A piece of proto-dynastic age from Faras in Nubia is in the Sudan Room at the Ashmolean Museum. The largest piece is the XVIIIth Dynasty sphinx (MASPERO, *Guide to the Cairo Museum*, fifth English edition, p. 130), but this is of opaque quartz, not crystal, and is glazed white.

[2] See the bead cases of these dates in the Ashmolean Museum, and Edwards Collection.

[3] These can all be studied in the bead cases of the Ashmolean Museum.

material from El Mahasna of VIth to XIth
Dynasty date.   Hence, with regard to this
quality of glaze, and to the melon beads themselves, and so many other details of Egyptian
civilization, it must be realised that it is not
peculiar to any given period, but that it has a
long history, coming into greatest prominence
in some one period, to which it is often
(wrongly) said to be peculiar.

A cylinder bead, type 17, was found, of good
blue glaze, with a black line winding round it in
a spiral from end to end.   This is a XIIth
Dynasty type, and is perhaps a decadent imitation in glaze of the old gold beads of the pre-
dynastic age[1] and of the IVth to Vth Dynasties.[2]
These again are probably related to such beads
as those of the proto-dynastic age, which are
made of gold wire coiled spirally.[3]

Black glaze was also much in fashion (Pl. III,
no. 3, Pl. VIII, nos. 3, 9, 10), and, as has been
remarked above, strikingly differentiates between
the pan-graves and those of the New Kingdom,
where similarly shaped beads are often made
of black glass, more or less transparent, and
showing bubbles in its substance.   In tomb
group B 222 (Pl. III, 3), these black glaze
spheroid beads were found with similar beads
of blue glaze.   This combination was found again
in the New Kingdom group B 108.

Blue frit was used in B 153 for spheroid
beads, type 10, see Pl. VIII, no. 17.   The use
of this material is known as early as the XIIth
Dynasty for spheroid beads and model *Conus*
shells, both of which can be seen in the
Ashmolean Museum.

---

[1] P., *L.G.M.*, Pl. v.

[2] GARSTANG, *El Mahásna and Bét Khalláf*, Pl. xxxvii.

[3] P., *R.T.*, ii, Pl. i, 3, and p. 18 ; DE MORGAN, *Tombeau Royal de Négadah*, fig. 744.

CHAPTER IV.

OBJECTS MADE OF LEATHER.

Plates IX, X, XI.

SANDALS.

Plate IX, 1. Sandals, or remains of them, were found in graves B 218, 222, 226, 227, 234, 243. All have one characteristic which distinguishes them from those of the New Kingdom, for they invariably consist of a single thickness of leather, and not several, as do the New Kingdom examples which we found. Moreover, they were all square or rounded at the toes, and never pointed, as so often in the New Kingdom. The New Kingdom sandal from B 170, Pl. XVIII, serves very well to illustrate both points. The leather of the pan-grave sandals is not reinforced by nails or by any other means. In types 1 and 3, which include the majority of the sandals, they were fastened by a toe-strap, springing from a single hole in the sole and passing back to a pair of loops at the ankle. How the strap was treated after this is not clear, and what evidence there is is not easy to interpret in the light of our knowledge of Egyptian sandals. In B 234 the toe-strap itself continues through the eyelet-hole in the ankle-strap, and, one supposes, must therefore finally either have been tied on itself over the instep, or have passed back to the hole in the toe whence it sprang. Both these arrangements would be contrary to those shown in the models,[1] and to those of actual specimens found in the XIth Dynasty temple of Deir el Bahri,[2] and at Kerma,[3] and also to those of most

of the drawings of sandals with a strap passing round behind the foot. In all these the toe-strap is separate from that round the foot, and ends in a loop on the instep through which the latter runs (fig. 6).[4]

The only true exceptions we have found to the general rule are the sandals carried behind Narmer on the great slate palette from Hierakonpolis.[5] Here, besides other minor variations from the general later type, the toe-straps do not exhibit any loop at the instep, but are themselves double (fig. 7). The fastening, therefore, is apparently carried out by a single strap

Fig. 6.

Fig. 7.

---

[1] PETRIE, *Deshasheh*, Pl. xxxiv, 6.

[2] See Pl. X.

[3] *Boston Museum of Fine Arts Bulletin*, vol. xii, fig. 20.

[4] A study of a number of examples shows that unless more evidence be forthcoming such apparent exceptions as nos. 411, 414, 418 of LACAU, *Sarcophages*, Pl. l, must be regarded as less detailed drawings of such sandals as are shown in SCHÄFER, *Priestergräber des Ne-user-rê*, fig. 73, Pl. xi. c, fig. 139, where the toe-strap is shown quite plainly to be separate from the strap which encircles the foot. It must be added that even if nos. 411, 414, 418 represented that which they seem to do, *i.e.* a single strap slit and passing through loops in the ankle-straps, such a system would not be applicable in our case, for the holes in our ankle-straps have never been open, as they are not looped but are eyelet-holes pierced in the strap itself. Thus they are only suited for the purpose of threading a loose end, and not for being fastened over an endless strap. These figures might, however, represent sandals in which the two ends of the encircling strap meet before passing into the hole at the toe. If so, they would represent that which we suggest to have been the method employed for our pair. However, the doubling of the part of the strap over the instep is never suggested at all, even in large drawings like those of N., *B.H.*, iv, Pl. xxvii, 1.

[5] QUIBELL, *Ä.Z.*, 36, Pls. xii, xiii.

starting from the toe of the sandal and running
round the foot back again to the toe.[1] Further
evidence can be adduced that this was the ancient
method, by the fact that detailed drawings of
the sign of life ☥ (ʿnḫ or ankh) show it double
at the "handle" or loose end. Battiscombe
Gunn has shown this sign to have originally
represented the sandal-strap, and Gardiner[2]
notes that it is difficult to make the Middle
Kingdom representations of the sandals and the
☥ tally in detail. He explains the difference on
the ground of the antiquity of the sign, and
from the evidence of Narmer's sandals this
is probably correct.[3] Thus from the details of
the ☥ hieroglyph, or ancient sandal-strap, we get
corroborative proof that the proto-dynastic
sandal was fastened by one continuous strap
springing from the toe, passing round behind
the foot, and returning to the toe again. Hence
it may be supposed that this was the means
employed in the case of B 234. In other words,

[1] The broad piece across the instep is no doubt some
sort of guard to prevent the strap chafing. In later times
the straps themselves were often made broad over the
instep. Cf. especially the unusual sandal in NEWBERRY,
The Life of Rekhmara, Pl. xvii, 3rd register.

[2] *Dictionary of Religion and Ethics*, "Life and Death,"
p. 21.

[3] The cross-pieces of the ☥ still offer a difficulty, for they
cannot represent a bow-tie on the instep, as no such thing
is ever found. From a study of originals, models, and
drawings, it is evident that what looks like the end of a
bow-tie on the instep of figs. 7, 8, 9 in Gardiner's article,
is really the toe-strap and its loop to which the rest of the
straps join. The cross-pieces of the ☥ should then be the
ankle-straps, though placed a little far forward in the
general scheme. In fig. 2 of that article they are actually
shown as slit for the eyelet-hole and bound with a strip of
leather, as were ours (cf. Pls. III, 3, VI, 1 and 2). Or we
might by the analogy of Narmer's sandals explain them as
some sort of a pad to relieve the instep. The line dividing
the two straps at the toe is quite clear in Quibell's drawing (*Ä.Z.*, 36, Pl. xiii), and in the original photograph
(*Hierakonpolis*, i, Pl. xxix). Its presence greatly increases
the similarity between the ☥ and the ancient sandal-straps.

[4] See Plates III, 3, VI, 2.

[5] LACAU, *Sarcophages*, i, *passim*.

to be white in the Pyramid Texts.[1] In one of
the coloured pictures of outfits for the dead man
two pairs of sandals are shown, one of which is
black and the other white.[2] Perhaps these
represent an every-day and a better pair.

Type no. 2 of Pl. IX is very different from
types 1 and 3. both in shape, manner of fastening,
and quality of leather. It is square toed, is not
shaped to fit the right or left foot, has two holes
for toe-straps instead of one, has no ankle-straps,
but is pierced with two holes towards the heel.
It would, therefore, seem to have been fastened
by two straps running from the toe to the heel,
and perhaps crossing on the instep. However,
we do not know exactly such a type elsewhere in
Egypt, though it may be connected with the
rather different sandals represented in the
wooden model of Middle Kingdom date.
Though this is not quite the same, for while
having the two holes near the heel it has only
one at the toe.[3] Again, it may be derived from
some such type as the strange form dating to
the beginning of the pre-dynastic period, S.D. 32.[4]
This pre-dynastic specimen, however, is much
more closely allied to the elaborate form adopted
by Absha's Aamu in the XIIth Dynasty,[5] and to
the unusual form of which only fragments
remain,[6] and which from the style of dress is
probably of Vth Dynasty date. With this
sandal, B 218, was found the bundle of cords—a
belt?—figured on Pl. X, 1.

Types of Leather.

We now come to the leather-work, examples
of which in some form or other were produced
by the majority of the graves, as a glance at the

[1] Sethe, *Pyr.*, § 1215, a.

[2] Schäfer, *Priestergräber des Ne-user-ré*, fig. 83, p. 59.

[3] *Ibid.*, fig. 159, p. 100.

[4] P., *D.P.*, Pl. x, 19.

[5] N., *B.H.*, i, Pl. xxxi.

[6] Petrie, *Medum*, Pl. xxviii, 6.

[7] Cf. the C-group leather; *A.S.N.*, 1907–08, p. 295, no. 24, no. 222.

The finer leather of chamois type, mostly in
very small pieces only a few inches square
stitched together to make a large piece, was
found in close contact with and following the
creases of the stouter skins.[1] It had certainly
lain under the latter at the time of burial,
though, unfortunately, it was all too brittle and
in fragments too small for us to see whether
the connection were any closer. As a rule it
came away quite freely from the skins, and it
had certainly not been closely attached to them
over its whole surface. However, in B 179,
where we found a large piece, it had been sewn
on to the skin, at one edge at least.[2] The other
edge had disappeared. At first we took the
finer leather to be the remains of a bag, but it
would have been too large to have been con-
venient ; therefore it is quite possible it was a
lining to the skin, stitched to it only here and
there.

This soft leather was sometimes ornamented
with little blue beads of type 3.[3] A great deal
of it was dyed red, notably in graves B 177,
179, 180, 201, 213, 226, 243, though only in
one instance, B 183, was red dye used on a skin
with the hair still on. One cannot but compare
this fine red-dyed leather with the material of
the long costumes worn by the Libyans (?) of
Beni Hasan,[4] and painted a dull red colour,
which evidently represents a similar leather.
In the fifth century B.C. the Libyan women were
still wearing a fringed costume of red-dyed
leather from which the hair had been removed,[5]

---

[1] See Pl. XI, 1, and found again in nos. B 177, 213.

[2] Cf. Pl. XI, 1, especially the top right-hand corner.

[3] See Pl. III, 2.

[4] N., *B.H.*, i, Pl. xlv. These figures are generally taken
to be Libyans on account of the feathers, no doubt, but
they are very different from the usual representatives of
these people. Appearing as they do in the XIIth Dynasty,
just before the pan-grave people are known in Egypt, and
wearing the pan-grave red leather garments, we may well
ask whether these are not pictures of pan-grave people.

[5] HERODOTUS, iv, 189.

the two are tightly stitched together by a leather thread passing through closely placed holes. Fig. 8. Until unpicked the seam has the appearance of having been riveted.

3. By causing the two edges to overlap considerably, and fastening each down by a row of coarse simple stitches at each edge.[1]

As a rule the stitchery is very good, and how neat the resulting join appeared on the outside can be judged from the example in the top right-hand corner of Pl. XI, 1. The thread used consisted of very finely cut strands of leather, and, as no needles were found, the leather was presumably pierced by means of the bone and copper awls frequent in the graves.[2]

· VARIOUS OBJECTS OF LEATHER.

Plate IX, 2. B 216, from a circular grave. A leather skirt found in position, the belt consisting of a cord wound three times round the waist. A similar arrangement was found in B 219, where a cord was twisted six times round the waist, supporting the costume, which was represented by a few fragments of leather tucked in under the belt.

Plate X, 1. Various examples of leather-work. No. B 219, from a circular grave, has white beads (type 1) sewn into the seams, as was the case in no. B 231, a long grave. A strip of leather has been inserted in the centre of the seam between the beads so as to keep the two rows apart. This garment was further ornamented on the surface with a fringe, as also was that of B 231. Hence, no doubt, the other fringed piece on the right-hand side of the photograph also originally belonged to it, though it was broken up and scattered in the plundered grave. The fringes are stitched in and thickly cover the surface of the leather. It

---

may be that the linen garments covered with loose hanging threads, which are sometimes worn in the New Kingdom, are a derivative of some such costume as this. The fringed leather costumes of the pan-graves seem to have belonged to women, since grave B 219 contained a *kohl*-pot, and was therefore probably that of a female, while the skeleton in B 231 was of this sex. One is thus reminded of the skirts of long leather fringes which the girls wear in Nubia and the Sudan at present, though to-day the fringes hang direct from the waist and are not set on a backing of leather. Unfortunately no evidence was forthcoming as to how the pan-grave fringed leather was used, whether as a skirt or a cloak.

Nos. B 225, 239, from two circular graves. Scraps of plaited or woven leather, presumably used as cords. No. B 239 had been manufactured flat and since rolled up longitudinally; this is clearly shown in Plate VII, 2.

No. B 214, from a circular grave. A piece of the ordinary stout leather cordage as found in B 177, 182A, 183, 214, 216, 219, 223, 224, 235, 239. Other examples will be found on Plates VII, 2, IX, 2, XI, 2. It is a plain twist, and should be compared with the narrower quality from B 218 figured alongside, and with the very fine quality found occasionally, as in B 235 (Pl. XI, 2), B 238, where it was used for the three anklets, and B 201, where two such fine cords fastened the wrist-guard or bracer. The piece under discussion also shows one of the knots used. For another, see the top of the bundle of cords alongside.

No. B 218, from a circular grave. A bundle of leather cords bound together in various places. It no doubt formed a belt, and is not unlike belts sometimes used to-day.

Plate X, 2. B 184, from a long grave. B 213, from an oval grave. See Pl. IV, 2, p. 11. Pierced leather-work of the same quality of stout leather as the skirt, Pl. IX, 2, and the leather, Pl. X, 1. B 184 was actually found on

---

[1] See Pl. XI, 1.

[2] See Plates II, 2, IV, 1, VII, 4.

the thigh, while in B 213, which was badly
wrecked, it was found near the pelvis. They
are thus the remains of leather kilts, and were
worn by men. Scraps of similar leather came
from B 225, a circular grave. Piereed leather
came from male graves of the C-group in
Nubia.[1] The fashion of wearing pierced leather
kilts may have given rise to the protective kilts
of slit leather so often worn over the ordinary
linen kilt by peasants in the New Kingdom.[2]
The ornamentation of our specimens by means of
small slits is very carefully and accurately done.
In B 213, the best preserved specimen, it
consists, in the middle pieee, of a margin of ten
continuous rows of slits succeeded by a similar
space filled with eight intermittent rows of slits
in groups of three with an occasional fourth.
In the right-hand piece, also from B 213, there
are thirteen continuous rows and eight intermittent. In this latter piece the spaces allotted
to the continuous and intermittent rows are
about the same, but are wider than the
corresponding ones in the middle piece. A
similar design, though different in details, is
exhibited in B 184. Here on one side a wide
space is occupied by at least seventeen continuous
rows, while a comparatively narrow space is

---

[1] *A.S.N.*, 1908–09, p. 60, no. 12, &c. See also p. 12.

[2] NEWBERRY, *The Life of Rekhmara*, Pl. xiii, lowest
register. Note the kilts worn by the men on the top
register of Pl. xxi, which have every appearance of being
different from the previous examples, and of being simply
leather pierced ornamentally as were our kilts. For larger
copies of both of these, see PRISSE, *Histoire de l'Art
égyptien*, ii, Pls. 58, 59.

[3] Cf. *A.S.N.*, 1907–08, p. 164, nos. 81, 85, 86, &c.;
A.S.N., 1909–10, p. 110, no. 68; p. 139, no. 451, where the
pillows are stuffed with chopped straw.

CHAPTER V.

VARIOUS TYPES OF OBJECTS.

Plates XII and XIII.

Plate XII, 1, 2, and 3 (B 201, 226, 235). See also Pl. III, 2, no. 12, and Pl. VI, 1. There can be little doubt that these objects are the archers' wrist-guards, or bracers, used to save the skin of the left forearm from the chafing of the released bow-string. . For, in the first place, the two decorated specimens include bows prominently among their patterns, and it should be noted that the groups of bows on B 201 are not nine in number, and so are merely ornamental and do not represent the traditional enemies of Egypt. In the second place, they were not found in pairs, but singly, as one would expect of bracers. The only possible exception is no. 2. However, this would seem to be a cover for the other rather than an actual guard, as it was found covering it and is made of thin leather, now very pliable, instead of the thick hide of the others ; further, it has a small hole in the point as if for the purpose of tying on to something. Against this cover theory must be set the difference in patterns on the cover and the covered. Bracers not unlike these are occasionally represented on the monuments. The earliest we know is a curiously shaped yellow object, which is just the shape of a side-view of such a bracer as ours when curved to fit the arm.[1]

A strange name is given, ⌐⌐ ⌐⌐ 𝓈𝓌ᶜ𝒷𝓌 (swabu). It is probable that the single bracelet which the archer wears on the wrist of his bow-hand in a Middle Kingdom tomb at Meir repre-

sents such a guard.[2] Later we find a definite example of the date of Amenhotep II,[3] where two bracers occur among a great collection of arms in a fresco. Rameses II is often shown wearing one on the left or extended arm.[4]

As regards the decoration, it will be noticed that the scheme has a generic resemblance in the two examples, for a lotus fills each of the top corners, which is barred off from the rest of the field by a series of straight lines. Unfortunately the upper central pattern of no. 3 is quite invisible. Underneath comes a decoration of wavy lines, which is followed by a bow or bows. The long tail is filled up by line patterns. The decorations have been pressed into the surface by means of a fairly blunt tool, which makes a good broad line. The marks sometimes ended in a spot, as in the ends of the lines of the lotus in the left-hand corner of no. 1. The area is outlined by two lines running round the edge, as was done in the case of the sandals. The bow figures conspicuously in the decoration. The representations are in the usual Egyptian fashion, showing a recurved weapon, a shape proper to the composite bow, which type,

---

[1] LACAU, *Sarcophages*, i, Pl. xli, fig. 225, and p. 179.

[2] BLACKMAN, *Rock Tombs of Meir*, i, Pl. vi.

[3] LEPSIUS, *Denkmäler*, iii, 64 a.

[4] CHAMPOLLION, *Monuments*, xiii = ROSELLINI, *Monumenti Storici*, lxxxi ; BUDGE, *The Egyptian Sudan*, ii, plate accompanying p. 324, though the bracer is lacking, as are many other minor details in the copies of this scene in C., *M.*, lxxi = R., *M.S.*, lxxiv. Cf. also C., *M.*, xi = R., *M.S.*, lxxix ; C., *M.*, xvii = R., *M.S.*, lxxxiii ; L., *D.*, iii, 176 d = C., *M.*, lxxiii = R., *M.S.*, lxiv.

however, does not appear in Egypt until the
XVIIIth Dynasty. It is a strange fact that
the regular Egyptian bow, from pre-dynastic
days onwards, was a simple one of plain wood,
though it usually had the double curve of the
composite bows.[1] Specimens can be seen in
many museums, for instance in the Ashmolean,
Case I, 53. It is still used to-day in Somali-
land.[2] Another but rarer type was known with
a single but often unsymmetrical curve.[3] Bows
with a single symmetrical curve are carried in the
XIIth Dynasty.[4] In the large representation on
our wrist-guard, as in others, the curve is
slightly exaggerated.

The central panel of no. 1 is filled with a
strange device like scales. It can hardly represent the common feather pattern, as this is
always turned the other way. In the triangular
tail space we have a water pattern in the one
case, and a diaper in the other. The two rows
of blocked-out triangles edging out a space are
well known in the ornamental leather work of
the XVIIIth Dynasty. The bracers were fastened
over the arm by a pair of fine leather cords in
the case of nos. B 201, 235, and a pair of fine
leather straps in the case of B 226, the remains
being still visible in Pl. VI, 1.

Plate XII, 4. See also Pls. II, 1; IV, 1; VII, 2.
Type of rounded potsherd, from round graves
B 110, 212, 229, and long grave B 208. The
edges were smoothed off all round, and the
sherds would thus appear to have been used as
scrapers or diggers. There is a curious uni-
formity about the shape, three of the four being
oval, while the fourth was more circular. They

GARSTANG, *Burial Customs of Ancient Egypt*, fig. 160,
p. 159.

[2] PAULITSCHKE, *Ethnographic Nordost-Africas*, Pl. xix,
fig. 61. A specimen is exhibited in the Pitt-Rivers
Museum at Oxford.

[3] As for instance LACAU, *Sarcophayes*, i, Pl. xli, nos. 230
to 234, where both shapes and a number of varieties of the
recurved bows are shown.

[4] N., *B.H.*, i, Pl. xlvii, &c.

B 227. See also Pls. III, 2: VI, 2, VII, 2, and pp. 10, 13. For shape this should be compared with the penannular objects of tortoise-shell of C-group date,[1] though the section of these, so far as can be seen, is quite different from that of our objects. Our specimens were all exactly alike, and no explanation of their use is forthcoming. We have offered the suggestion that they were strigils or body-scrapers, and have compared them (p. 13) to the curved skewer of hard wood or ibex-horn that the desert Hamite of to-day wears in his hair.

Plate XII, 9. A piece of horn of rounded section from the oval grave B 213. See also p. 12. It was found with the net bag of elephant's hair and the pierced leather (Pl. IV, 2). It cannot well have been a bracelet, unless it has sprung out of shape, for at present its curvature is too slight. Though in curve it resembles no. 8, yet in section it is quite different.

Plate XII, 10. Tortoise-shell bracelet from long grave B 201. See Pl. III, 2, and p. 10.

Plate XIII, 1, 2. Types of copper axes from long graves B 201, 230, and circular grave B 226. See also Pls. III, 2, VI, 1, and pp. 10, 12. It is to be observed that both examples of type 1 were found in long graves, while type 2 came from a circular grave. Type 1 is very much lighter than type 2, as will be seen by a comparison of their respective side-views. Both these types afterwards became usual in the New Kingdom; but while no. 2 is known in the XIIth Dynasty,[2] no. 1 is not. Type 1 would seem to be of Intermediate Period and XVIIIth Dynasty date,[3] and does not appear to run back into the XIIth Dynasty.[4] Hence its appearance in history would seem to be some-

---

[1] *A.S.N.*, 1908–09, Pl. 37 c, 9.

[2] P., *D.P.*, Pl. xxxii, 3; P., *K.G.H.*, Pl. xvii, 6, 9.

[3] P., *D.P.*, Pl. xxxii, notably no. 22; P., *G.R.*, Pl. xii, stated to be early XVIIIth Dynasty on p. 14; BISSING, *Thebanischer Grabfund*, Pl. 1, the axe of Ahmose.

[4] Cf. P., *D.P.*, pp. 51, 52.

[5] Cf. BISSING, *Thebanischer Grabfund*, Pl. xii, nos. 8, 9; *Archaeologia*, 53, Part i, Pl. iii, fig. 2.

[6] See Pl. VI, 1; QUIBELL, *Ramesseum*, Pl. ii, 7.

[7] P., *D.P.*, Pl. xxxii, 21.

[8] BISSING, *Thebanischer Grabfund*, Pl. i; cf. Pl. xi; *Archaeologia*, 53, Pl. iii, no. 2, &c.

features of no. 2 are seen in its early forms in the XIIth Dynasty. At present there seems to be a long gap in its history, for with the exception of our specimens it does not occur again till the later New Kingdom, when it becomes common.[1]

Plate XIII, 3. No. B 201/7, from a long grave. See also Pl. III, 2, and p. 10.

Plate XIII, 4. No. B 205 from a long grave, and B 226 from a circular grave. See also Pl. VI, 1, and p. 12. The pair of tweezers from B 226 was ornamented with two cuts, while that from B 205 was plain.

Plate XIII, 5–9. See p. 19 and Pl. VIII, 1, no. 16, for nos. 7, 8, 9.

Plate XIII, 10. Type of white shell earring. See Pl. VII, 1, and p. 13.

Plate XIII, 11. A melon bead. Nos. B 153, 201/10, from long graves; B 236, from a pan-grave group. See Pl. VIII, 1, nos. 12, 16; cf. III, 2, no. 10.

Plate XIII, 12, 13, 14. See also Pls. II, 2, III, 2, VI, 1, and pp. 9, 10, 12. Nos. B 201, 207, 208 came from long graves; B 232 came from a unique oval (?) grave with a step, which is perhaps only an unfinished long grave; B 219, 226 came from circular graves. It is noticeable that out of the six *kohl*-pots discovered half came from long graves, and possibly B 232 should be included in this category, as it was more rectangular than oval in shape. Only two were found in the more numerous circular graves. Two came from graves nos. B 201, 226, which included weapons, axes and bracers, and were therefore those of men. The blackening of the eyelids by men is still customary in Egypt, especially at festivals, and has been adopted as a Mohammedan ordinance. Two of the *kohl*-pots from graves B 208/10, 232 were of blue marble,

---

[1] P., *L.G.M.*, Pl. xxii, 12, p. 28; P., *K.G.H.*, Pl. xvii, 27, 28; QUIBELL, *Ramesseum*, Pl. ii, 7, p. 13; PETRIE, *Dendereh*, Pl. xxiv, 16, 17; MACIVER, *El Amrah and Abydos*, Pl. xlv, D 1.

[2] At Sawâmah last year we found a specimen. Cf. GAR-STANG, *El Arabah*, p. 29, where three cases are quoted: CURRELLY, *Abydos*, iii, Pl. lix, 5, 6.

[3] P., *K.G.H.*, Pl. xiv, 16.

Plate XIII, 15, 20. See also Pls. II, 2, VI, 1, and pp. 9, 12. Specimens of small smooth stones or pebbles, of which quite a number, of varying sizes, were found, some, like the agate and four black pebbles in B 213, being quite small. None were large. They came from graves B 208, 213, 223, 226.

Plate XIII, 16, 17, 18, 19. See also Pls. II, 1, VI, 1, VII, 2, and pp. 8, 12, 13. Several palettes were found with paint or signs of rubbing on them. In B 110 there were two (nos. 16, 17 in this Plate), with one rubber nearly as large as themselves. These two palettes consisted of flat natural pebbles of black granite, while their rubber was a rounded pink pebble. From this grave also came the notched pebble no. 19, which had a few longitudinal scratches, and so might have been a palette, though it showed no

---

[1] *A.S.N.*, 1907–08, Pl. 66, b, 32.

CHAPTER VI.

THE POTTERY.

Plates V

THE pan-grave pottery forms a very distinctive class, and so far as Egypt is concerned it is quite apart from anything else. Each of the pan-grave sites has produced at least a few examples of the stock types, except that at Balabish we did not find any of the black punctured ware, and at Rifeh comparatively little of the Buff ware seems to have been used. The general similarity of the *corpora* of pan-grave pottery is apparent on a comparison of our Pls. V and XIV with *Diospolis Parva*, Pls. xxxix, xl, and *Gizeh and Rifeh*, Pls. xxv, xxvi. It will be observed that the native-made classes P, B, and H are all bowls. We did not find any of the beautiful black-topped cups with flared rims and a grey band, for the reason to be explained on p. 43. The types are all drawn on Pl. XIV, and examples are photographed on Pl. V, to show the quality, surface, and so on.

1. *Red Polished Ware*, *P*; cf. Pl. V, nos. 242, 182A. This is a rare fabric, of which we found only the three specimens figured. It is a very fine quality pottery, with a brilliant red-polished surface. The walls are very thin, as hard as stone, and show a black core on a fracture with a little sand in the clay, but never any chopped straw (*tibn*). The photographs of nos. B 242, 182A, on Pl. V, 1, show the quality of the material. The shape of P 3 is rare and is not easy to match. Among Egyptian pottery we can compare it in shape with two vases alone, one from Abydos,[1] of Late Inter-

---

[1] P., *C.A.*, ii, Pl. xxxi.

[2] QUIBELL, *Excavations at Saqqara*, 1906-07, Pl. xxxix, 1.

[3] *A.S.N.*, 1907-08, Pl. 60, a, 13.

[4] *A.S.N.*, 1907-08, Pl. 61. a, 22; *A.S.N.*, 1908-09 Pl. 44, a, no. 1.

[5] R. N. BRADLEY, *Malta and the Mediterranean Race*, fig. 31 (opposite p. 142), the smaller of the two here figured.

to the rim, and never descended .far over the
surface of the pot. When it is not otherwise
indicated by a wavy line it coincides with the
rim. We suspect that the taste for painting a
black rim on red pottery, which came in in the
XVIIIth Dynasty, is a reminiscence of these
pan-grave pots. In the pan-grave pottery the
black is of a brilliant metallic lustre, and the
interior of the pots is black. The polishing of
the specimen from B 181 was exceptionally fine,
the colour being a handsome rich plum-red.
Though the polish on some of the others was
more brilliant, it was not so even as on this. This
can be seen by a comparison of the photographs
on Pl. V. The colour as a rule was a good red.
It should be observed that the apparent grey
ring on B 181 in the photograph is not an
integral part of the pot, but is only due to
an incrustation of salt.

Type 8 probably does not belong to this class
at all, as it was of a thick coarse manufacture
and black all over. Its clay had some sand in
it, but, like the others, did not contain chopped
straw. As we only once found fragments of
such a vessel we have tentatively included it
here, in preference to making a separate class
for it alone.

The deep straight-sided bowls are common in
the pan-graves, and are found in other burials
of the Intermediate Period,[1] but in this last case
the ware is entirely different, being of a soft
ochre material. The moulding at the rim seems
to be peculiar to the pan-grave pottery, and is
not very common even in that of the Nubian
C-group.[2] The collar of nos. 4, 5, 6 resembles
that on pottery of the early ages, late pre-
dynastic or proto-dynastic times. It seems
just to last into the Old Kingdom, when it dies
out.[3] The rare shape of no. 6, with the un-
curved sides expanding towards the bottom,

[4] *A.S.N. Bull.*, no. 6, pp. 3, 5, class xi; cf. *A.S.N.*,
1909–10, p. 19. The other classes of C-group incised
ware are not comparable to our bowls, as in class xii the
clay is quite different, being soft, and in class iv not only
is the clay of another quality, but the vessels themselves
and ornaments differ completely.

[5] P., *N.B.*, Pl. xxxv, 74, 76.

[6] Cf. P., *K.G.H.*, Pl. xiii, nos. 106, 108, and our H 2.

[7] For instance, P., *K.G.H.*, Pl. xiii, 39 ff.; *G.R.*,
Pl. xiii D, 170, 181, xxv, 11, 12, but on this plate cf. the
rare bowl 41.

[1] P., *C.A.*, ii, Pl. xxix, C 63, pp. 60, 64.

[2] For references, see p. 47.

[3] For references, see p. 47.

The hatching was produced by a blunt point or group of points on the surface after it had dried, but before firing. The incisions seem to have been made singly, though the pit markings on the moulding of B 240 (see Pl. V) seem to be too regular to have been produced in any way but by the use of a comb. The rows of pit markings vary somewhat in the number of marks included, those on B 240 ranging from seven to nine, while those on the bowl figuring as type 4 range from five to six. The favourite pattern at Balabish consists of opposing to each other sets of arcs of concentric circles (types 2, 4, 5), and the same idea is carried out in straight lines and amplified in type 3.

4. *Buff Ware.* Cf. Pl. V, no. 212. A very unmistakable class of pottery, very well made of a thick, hard, close, fine clay, and well turned. The colour varied somewhat from a pinkish yellow to almost a pink, but the yellowish tinge preponderated. It was liable to go green, especially if it had contained scented ointment. The beautifully smooth silky surface which one connects with the best quality cylinder jars of the Ist Dynasty[1] was observed on some of the pots, especially on nos. B 201/3, 4, and 233, which contained ointment. Probably therefore this effect is partly produced by the oily nature of the ointment, and is not merely due to the clay itself, especially as it was found on the two pots from B 201, which were different from the others in being red-polished. The clay is close and entirely without chopped straw, but contains a good deal of sand, and is thus not unlike that of the W or D classes of pre-dynastic pottery, and some of the proto-dynastic ware, but the colour is much yellower. It is a variety of the pottery which Reisner calls class ' C.[2] The massive rims of these thick, strong pre-dynastic classes occur in the pan-grave pottery again,[3] and

---

[1] P., *N.B.*, Pl. xxxii, 71 a, 80.   [2] *N.D.*, ii, p. 90.

[3] P., *N.B.*, Pl. xxxi, 14/33; xxxiv, 47, 51; and our types 4, 7, 8, 9.

[4] PETRIE, *Abydos*, iii, Pl. lx, 127.

[5] Such as PETRIE, *Abydos*, iii, Pl. lx, 129; P., *L.G.M.* Pl. xvii, 19.

[6] P., *D.P.*, Pls. xxxix, xl.

below it in the Plate. In view of the general homogeneity of this class and the resemblances of its clay and rims to those of some classes of pre- and proto-dynastic pottery, it seems as if some extraneous influence were at work giving new life to an old industry which had languished. It is hardly likely that the arrival of the pan-grave people themselves should have given this fresh impetus, as in their homeland of Nubia this ware is only known as an import, and moreover this kind of pottery is in use in Egypt before the pan-grave period, as it dates back to the XIIth Dynasty. There is, however, another force which may well be accountable for the revival of the old art. This is the influence of Asia. Egypt was in close connection with Asia during the middle pre-dynastic period, when the use of this clay was first introduced with the wavy-handled and decorated classes of pottery. This is evidenced by the use of such materials as lapis-lazuli,[1] silver,[2] emery,[3] obsidian,[4] &c. In

the proto-dynastic age Asiatic influence is once more noticeable, and this is the time of the cylinder jars, the clay of which, with its silky drab surface, closely resembles that of our class of ware, and is in fact more exactly similar than any other class of Egyptian pottery. In the proto-dynastic age obsidian[5] is not uncommon as a material for vases, lapis-lazuli[6] is used again, art shows striking resemblances to that of Babylonia, a rare Ist Dynasty type of copper adze is found again in Cyprus,[7] and foreign pottery of a Syrian(?) character is found in

---

[1] P., *D.P.*, Pl. iv, p. 27. A large piece of lapis-lazuli of middle pre-dynastic age is recorded in P., *N.B.*, p. 28. Another, S.D. 56–64, *El Amrah and Abydos*, p. 21. In the XVIIIth Dynasty lapis-lazuli was obtained from N. Syria in general, and also from Assyria (B., *A.R.*, ii, § 446; WINCKLER, *Tell el Amarna Letters*, no. 15), Singara, in N. Mesopotamia (B., *A.R.*, ii, 484), Mitanni and Babylon (*Amarna Letters*, nos. 7, 9, 10, 17, 19, 21). A special quality is described as lapis-lazuli of Babylon (B., *A.R.*, ii, 446, 484). This all agrees with the supposition that its ultimate place of origin was Persia, which is still the main source of supply, and also is the least distant from Egypt.

[2] P., *D.P.*, Pl. iv, p. 27. A larger piece is to hand in the silver bowl of a spoon, S.D. 60–70, recorded in *El Amrah*, p. 24. For the sources, see p. 39, note 2. A silver dagger from Gebel el Tarif is probably of the middle pre-dynastic age also, for it was found in the same cemetery as painted pottery of class D (DE MORGAN, *Recherches sur les Origines de l'Égypte*, p. 35).

[3] For emery of the middle pre-dynastic period, see P., *N.B.*, Pl. lxiv, 99, p. 48. This piece was found with the bull's head amulet, Pl. lxi, 4, which is a middle pre-dynastic type. The emery blocks for polishing beads, p. 44, are presumably of this date also. The emery double vase, *Hierakonpolis*, ii, Pl. lxiv, 20, p. 50, is probably also of the middle pre-dynastic period, as the majority of the dateable

Egypt.[1] Similarly in the XIIth Dynasty, when Drab ware is found again, Asiatic products once more appear in the obsidian[2] and silver[3] so very

---

[1] P., *R.T.*, ii, Pl. liv; *Abydos*, i, Pl. viii. In these plates the pottery is provisionally described as Aegean, but this was before the discoveries in Crete. *Tarkhan*, i, Pls. xvi, xix, 24, p. 17, § 30.

For the original publication, DE MORGAN, *Fouilles à Dahchour*, 1894, 1894–5, should be consulted, but the information required here is conveniently grouped in MASPERO'S *Guide to the Cairo Museum* (QUIBELL'S translation), 1908, p. 426, A, various silver plaques; p. 427, B, silver settings to eyes from three mummy cases; p. 428, E, silver mirrors; three eye-settings in silver; p. 429, B, several silver mirrors (11 and 12 cm. in diameter and of thick metal); p. 431, F, a large diadem of silver. Besides these there are some very massive plates about 10 cm. long and various other large and massive objects not named in the Guide-book. Another group of silver jewellery of this age, including hawks and a bracelet, is figured in *El Amrah and Abydos*, Pl. xlv, and p. 88. A large number of silver vessels were dedicated to different gods by one of the Senuserts (DARESSY, *Ann. du Service*, iv, p. 102). Five vases of obsidian are named on p. 428, ii, of the Guide-book. Obsidian scarabs are said to be very characteristic of the XIIIth Dynasty (HALL, *Cat. of Egyptian Scarabs, &c., in the Brit. Mus.*, i, p. xxvi). Both the obsidian and the silver might be supposed to have come from the Aegean, as archaeologists chiefly think of obsidian as coming from Melos and other Greek islands where it is well known. Manufactured silver also is known at an early date from Crete (Mosso, *Palaces of Crete*, p. 271, fig. 132), from Amorgos (DÜMMLER, *Athen. Mitth.*, 1886, Beil. i, D 1, 3, p. 20), while in classical times silver was mined at Siphnos (*Hdt.*, iii, 57), on the borders of Macedonia (*Hdt.*, v, 17), and there were the famous mines at Laureion, near Athens (SMITH, *Dict. Greek and Roman Geography*, Laurium). But in view of the above-mentioned earlier occurrences in Egypt of these imports in clearly Asiatic connections, and in view of the strong connection that there is with Syria in the XIIth Dynasty (cf. the Sinuhe story, Senusert III's campaign in Retenu, El Arabah, p. 33), it seems quite unnecessary to go to the Aegean for the origin of these implements. For obsidian is largely used for neolithic implements in Russian Armenia (CHANTRE, *Recherches Anthropol. dans le Caucase*, i, fig. 2, Pl. i, figs. 1, 3, 5, 6, 7), and it was also used in prehistoric stations at Susa and in the neighbourhood of Mesopotamia (DE MORGAN, *Recherches sur les Origines de l'Égypte*, p. 175). Its abundance at the eastern end of Asia Minor and its neighbourhood makes unnecessary any idea of importation from so distant a place as the Aegean. Further, in ancient days silver was very definitely a product of Eastern Asia Minor and its neighbourhood. Tarshish (Tarsus) exported

it (Jer. x. 9; Ezek. xxvii. 12). Keftiu (Cilicia and its neighbourhood) exported silver ingots and blocks to Egypt (Rekhmire fresco, see *L.A.A.A.*, vi, p. 54). Shalmaneser II names a mountain in Tabal, the Antitaurus and Amanus district, which contained silver (E. SCHRADER, *Keilinschr. Bibl.*, i, 143). The Hittites brought silver to Egypt (B., *A.R.*, ii, § 485; SETHE, *Urk.*, iv, p. 701, l. 12); the metal presents of the Hittite king Shubbiluliuma consist entirely of silver (KNUDTZON, *Die el-Amarna Tafeln*, letter 41), and the seal of the Hittite treaty with Rameses II is also of silver (B., *A.R.*, iii, § 391; L., *D.*, iii, 146, l. 36). Tuthmosis III obtained large weights of silver from N. Syria on his fifth and seventh campaigns, and a silver statue from the Lebanon district, besides "silver in many rings" (B., *A.R.*, ii, 436, 459, 471; SETHE, *Urk.*, iv, p. 666, l. 9; p. 686, l. 6; p. 692, l. 1), while the following list of occurrences of silver objects or of objects ornamented with silver shows how general was its use throughout this country in the fifteenth cent. B.C. (B., *A.R.*, ii, §§ 431, 434, 435, 447, 462, 467, 482, 490, 491, 501, 509, 518, 533, 537). Hence it is not surprising that silver was called "northern," 𓊹𓏤𓈖 (SETHE, *Urk.*, iv, p. 634, nos. 8, 9). The Assyrian kings obtained great quantities of silver from the Amanus and N. Mesopotamian districts (E. SCHRADER, *Keil. Bibl.*, i, 67, 73, 75, 163, &c.). It is unnecessary to add the classical references also, but suffice it to say that silver mines are reported from E. Asia Minor to-day. This in conjunction with the other Asiatic connections above-named—lapis-lazuli, emery, art, similarity of adzes—leaves little doubt but that Egypt's earlier supply of obsidian and silver also came from Asia.

[3] See below, p. 67, note [2].

[4] Some of these N. Syrian vessels are published by WOOLLEY in *L.A.A.A.*, vi, Pls. xxii, xxiii.

ointment jars of the Buff ware to that of some
of the proto-dynastic cylinder jars. Out of the
six times that traces of ointment were discovered
they attached themselves in B 182, 182A, 201,
233, 240 to vessels of this ware. In the other
case, B 208, a strong scent of ointment per-
meated the whole pile of objects, which had
contained several pots of this class. However,
it did not attach itself to any single object more
than to another.

The use of this class of clay for pottery
destined to contain ointment is yet another link
between the pan-grave people and those of the
later pre- and proto-dynastic age.

Types 1 *to* 6. While these belong to the
general class of pear-shaped vases which has
representatives in almost all the earlier ages
of Egyptian civilization from the pre-dynastic
onwards, it is not easy to match some of the
specimens exactly outside of the pan-grave
period.

No. 1. We find no satisfactory connections
outside of the pan-graves. It is red-polished.

No. 2 is not unlike a contemporary vase
of the Intermediate Period,[1] but is still more
like the pan-grave example X, 48.[2] It is red-
polished.

No. 3 is not one of those which are found in
the pan-grave pottery of *Diospolis Parva*, and
perhaps has more resemblance to the Egyptian
shapes than the others. It might be compared to
such vases as *Dendereh*, Pl. xvii, 44 (VII–XIth
Dyns.); *Qurneh*, Pl. xviii, 468 (XIth Dyn.);
P., *D.P.*, Pl. xxxvi, 152 (XII–XVIIIth Dyns.);
P., *G.R.*, Pl. xxvii, J, 275 (Tuthmosis III); *Six
Temples at Thebes*, Pl. vii, 1 (Tuthmosis IV).

No. 4 resembles the XIIth Dynasty shape of
El Kab, Pl. xvii, 126, but more still the pot 83,
P., *G.R.*, Pl. xxvi, which is of the XVIth Dynasty,
and quite likely from a pan-grave.

No. 5. We have not found anything really

[3] PETRIE and others, *Meydum and Memphis III*, Pl. xxvii,
101; PETRIE, *Ehnasya*, Pl. xxxix, top row.

[4] P., *D.P.*, Pls. xiv, 67; xix, 59, *a*, *b*.

[5] PETRIE, *Dendereh*, Pl. xvii, 59 (VII–XIth Dynasties);
the EARL OF CARNARVON, *Explorations at Thebes*, Pl. xlvii,
no. I (Intermediate Period).

[6] P., *C.A.*, ii, Pl. xxxiii, B 15, p. 69. Attention must
be called in passing to the isolated specimen, *Abydos*, ii,
Pl. xliv, 97, dated to the IInd–Vth Dynasties. It has no
doubt got out of its horizon.

[7] See the previous reference; also PETRIE, *Abydos*, iii,
Pl. lx, 127, and often.

[1] MACIVER and MACE, *El Amrah and Abydos*, Pl. liv, 42.
[2] P., *D.P.*, Pl. xxxix.

El Arabah, Pl xx, E 268 or P., *G.R.*, Pl. xxvii, G 189.

5. *Borrowed Pottery.* This consists of quite a heterogeneous collection of shapes and clays.

Type 1 was burnished red in a poor streaky manner. The lines of burnishing did not run down to the centre of the bowl, but across in such a way as to divide the circle into four segments.

Type 2 is an ordinary pre-dynastic pot of type D 5b.[1] The clay has fired to an unusually green colour, and the decoration of wavy lines has been put on with the usual red paint. As mentioned on p. 9, isolated pre-dynastic pots have several times been found in the graves of the related C-group people of Nubia. There was evidently a taste for the products of this age.

---

[1] P., *N.B.*, Pl. xxxiii, 5, b.

[2] P., *G.R.*, Pls. xxv, xxvi; P., *C.A.*, ii, Pl. xxix, c, 63.

CHAPTER VII.

COMPARATIVE SURVEY OF THE PAN-GRAVE CIVILIZATION.

FROM the material found in the three published
pan-grave cemeteries, those of Hu, Rifeh and
Balabish, it is evident that the civilization
exhibited by them is one. Naturally, there are
differences between the three, as for instance the
presence of large black incised bowls at Hu and
the absence of such bowls from Rifeh and
Balabish, the presence of axes and wrist-guards
(bracers) at Balabish and their absence from Hu
and Rifeh, and so on. Yet these are only minor
differences, such as would be bound to occur
between separate sites, each of which produced
comparatively few graves. Perhaps more serious,
however, is the absence of burials of dogs and
beetles from both Rifeh and Balabish.[1] These
few differences, however, only tend to throw
into relief the homogeneity of the whole. Petrie
has already given a description of the pan-
grave civilization itself, which is to some extent
supplemented by our finds.

We did not find any of the beautiful flared
cups of thin red polished ware with black tops
and a grey band separating the black from the
red.[2] Not unnaturally, at the time of their
first discovery in Egypt they were included
among the objects from the newly discovered
pan-graves. This was the more natural, as
bowls of hatched ware not dissimilar from those
from the neighbouring pan-graves were found

---

[1] To these more serious differences must be added the
difference in the form of the graves, which at Hu were
shallow pans, whereas at Rifeh and Balabish they were
pits about 1·50 m. deep. The shallowness of the Hu
graves may perhaps be due to denudation.

[2] See P., D.P., Pl. xxxviii, top right-hand corner, or
MACIVER and WOOLLEY, Buhen, Pl. 52.

Nubia, just above the Third Cataract, whence come also an immense quantity of cups and bowls of this very unmistakable ware, though whether this pottery was actually found with these objects we are unable to say from Reisner's brief reports. Further, it should be pointed out that, apart from Abadiyeh and Kerma, these horn-protectors are unknown, so far as we are aware. This makes the double connection all the more remarkable. Again, Kerma produces large fly ornaments and daggers, all of precisely the same rather rare types found with these pots at yet another place—Wady Halfa. Returning to the *Diospolis Parva* plates, it will be further noticed that these beautiful bell-shaped black-topped cups, so often called pan-grave ware and classed as C-group, occur at Abadiyeh only in this unique grave, E 2. They are not found in any of the other plates [1] which illustrate the pure pan-grave civilization. They also differentiate themselves from the black-topped pottery found in the pan-graves by their exceptionally fine polish, by the ring of grey dividing the black from the red, and also by their shapes. They have already been shown to belong to a very definite class of objects, and the presumption, therefore, is that these delicate cups and their associated civilization are not pan-grave. Now inquiry shows that, though they have many times occurred in other horizons, they have only once been found with distinctive pan-grave objects, namely, at Wady Halfa, where the grave containing them also produced some of the true pan-grave shell strips for bracelets.[2] It also produced the dagger and flies, which are not pan-grave, but similar to those from Kerma.

The thin black-topped cups with flared rims and a grey band have been found at :—

1. Abydos, in a shaft tomb with chambers,

---

[1] P., *D.P.*, Pls. xxxix, xl; P., *G.R.*, Pls. xxv, xxvi, or in this volume.

[2] MacIver and Woolley, *Buhen*, p. 175.

and other vessels of the same pottery, were
found in such great quantities as to suggest that
the other sporadic finds are finally referable to
this civilization. Though at present we are not
in a position to say whether the pots and the
objects were actually found in the same graves,
it is at least significant that so many of the
objects already found elsewhere with this black-
topped pottery are once more found on the
same site. For here, at Kerma, once more are
found a dagger and flies similar to those of
Buhen (*Ä.Z.*, 1914, Taf. iv), and also knives
and objects seen to be rams' horn protectors [1]
(*Ä.Z.*, 1914, Taf. iv, vi, 12), similar to those
from grave E 2 at Abadiyeh (P., *D.P.*,
Pl. xxxviii). The knives from the two places
are not similar in type, but show that both
peoples used such implements. All these are
things that are not found in pan-graves.

Thus this people of the black-topped cups
with the flared rims and grey band would seem
to be neither the pan-grave people nor yet
ordinary C-group people. In Egypt they would
seem to have been a little later than the pan- [2]
grave people, hence it is not surprising that
we did not find these cups in our pan-grave
cemetery. A few points which may bear on
their connection with Egypt have been set out
on p. 7.

Having eliminated this civilization, we can
now proceed with the analysis of that of the [3]
pan-graves. Apart from borrowed objects, such
as the *kohl*-pots, tweezers, axes and pottery, the
pan-grave civilization is something quite distinct
so far as Egypt is concerned. While it shows
affinities to various others, the C-group of Nubia [4]
is the only one which can be said to be really
connected with it, and even here the connections
are mainly confined to the later phase of the
C-group period. The pan-grave civilization has
a certain resemblance to that of the pre-dynastic
peoples, primarily due to its use of contracted [5]

[1] See Pl. XIV, and p. 41.

[2] See the references on p. 9.

[3] P., *D.P.*, p. 48. The burial of dogs was an early pre-
dynastic custom, for it is reported from a grave datable to
S. D. 36 (P., *N.B.*, p. 26, no. 286), and on p. 13 of the
same volume it is reported with C pottery (polished red
pottery with white cross-lines), which died out in early
pre-dynastic times.

[4] *A.S.N.*, 1907–08, Pl. 60 a, no. 13.

[5] As reported in P., *D.P.*, p. 48. For the pre-dynastic
beetles, see p. 33 of the same volume.

[6] For references, see p. 9.

[7] P., *N.B.*, p. 11 ; PETRIE, *Tarkhan*, i, p. 9, &c.

skulls.[1] The veneration of these may well be
connected with that of another horned head of
this period, i.e., the stag's head sculptured on
the proto-dynastic Min-statue of Koptos.[2] These
same proto-dynastic statues exhibit yet another
resemblance to the pan-graves in the large shells,
which are usually very rare in Egypt, but which
here figure conspicuously among the sacred
emblems on all three statues.[3] The pan-graves,
in their fondness for small shells other than
cowries as ornaments resemble the early dynasties of Nubia,[4] and those of Egypt in their use
of gold imitation shells.[5] They also resemble
the pre-dynastic people in this respect (MacIver
and Mace, El Amrah and Abydos, p. 49), though
naturally such shells may be found occasionally
at other periods.

The use of glazed crystal is probably another
link with the pre- to proto-dynastic age, which
was the most flourishing period of the art.[6]

The sandals of the pan-grave people have been
seen to resemble those of the Narmer palette
more than any others.[7]

A variety of the pattern fig. 9 is used in the
pan-graves on the H pottery. This
pattern is not general in Egypt,
but occurs mostly on proto-dynastic
objects[8] and Middle Kingdom coffins.[9]

Fig. 9.

The bowl of type B 5 resembles in shape
pottery of the late pre- or proto-dynastic age.[10]

Passing to the different peoples and countries
to whom the pan-grave civilization shows
affinities, we notice :—

1. *Ancient Nubia.* In the large use it made
of shells bored for suspension the pan-grave
civilization resembles Ancient Nubia, where the
custom seems to have been common all through
the Early Dynastic and B-group periods,[16] though
it seems largely to have died out in C-group
times. To a limited extent such shells were

[1] P., *D.P.*, p. 48; P., *R.T.*, ii, Pl. vii, 8; *Tarkhan*, i,
Pl. ii, 4, where an ox skull is set on a shrine. This
survived late, associated in writing with the shrine of
Sebek at Crocodilopolis in the Fayum (for a sculptured
representation see P., *L.G.M.*, xxix), and it appears in the
XIXth Dynasty at Abydos, Caulfield, *The Temple of
the Kings at Abydos*, Pl. vii. For much information on
the whole subject of bucrania in Egypt see Lefébure,
Le Bucráne, Sphinx, x, pp. 67 ff.

[2] Petrie, *Koptos*, Pl. iii, 1.

[3] Petrie, *Koptos*, Pl. iii, 1, 2, 3.

[4] *A.S.N.*, 1907–08, volume of plates, p. 18, Pl. 66 E.

[5] R., *N.D.*, i, Pls. 6, 7, p. 139; cf. also Petrie, *Tarkhan*, ii,
Pl. xxxv, 1619, xxxvi, 1819, xlii, 763, 797, 1438; Junker,
Friedhof in Turah, Pl. xlix, b.

also used in the Egyptian proto-dynastic period.[1]

Another connection is to be found in the weaving of hair (giraffe's or elephant's?), of which we found a specimen at Balabish in the little bag, Pl. IV, 2, which art was practised at Kerma in Nubia.[2]

2. *Ancient Sudan.* In the use of hatched pottery and of a lip-stud the pan-graves resemble this country, for these ornaments have been found near Roseires on the Blue Nile, and also at Gebel Moya in the Senaar Province.[3] Another resemblance is probably to be seen in the braiding of the men's hair (see p. 11)

3. *Modern Sudan.* It resembles the modern Sudan in the use of clothing of fine leather thongs, and modern Abyssinia in the probable braiding of the men's hair, and also the Negroids of South Kordofan.[4] There is a further resemblance in the use of elephant's hair, for the natives of the Sudan make bracelets of this material to-day. The probable plaiting of a man's hair by the pan-grave people resembles the usage of Abyssinia.[5]

4. *Ancient Libyans.* It resembles these people in the use of red-dyed leather garments[6] and of fringed leather costumes.[7] The dressing of the hair in ridges(?) and plaits by the Libyans resembles the probable plaiting of a man's hair in the pan-graves,[8] and the decoration of the cross-bands of the Libyans seems to imply a connection with the shell-strip bracelets of the pan-grave people.[9]

---

[1] For references, see note 5 on p. 45.

[2] *A.Z.*, 1914, p. 37, no. 9.

[3] WELLCOME, *Report Brit. Ass.*, 1912, p. 617.

[4] Kindly communicated by Dr. Seligmann. For Abyssinia, see p. 11.

[5] For references, see p. 11.

[6] N., *B.H.*, i, Pl. xlv, if these figures actually are Libyans, as is usually supposed.

[7] HERODOTUS, iv, 189.

[8] For references, see p. 11.

[9] For references, see p. 20.

[10] P., *D.P.*, p. 26.

[11] *A.S.N.*, 1909–10, pp. 138–140.

though this change started in pre-
pan-grave times, p. 15, no. 3).

(b)

3. *Ashes.*

The pan-graves never deposit ashes.
The earlier C-group deposits ashes (*A.S.N.*
1909–10, pp. 18, 19).

4. The pottery of the pan-graves shows many
differences from that of the C-group.

(*a*) *Quality.*

Our pan-grave pottery of each of the
P, B and H classes was singularly
free from chopped straw, and was
remarkable for its thinness, the majority
of the walls being about 3 mm. in
thickness, but varying from 2 to 4 mm.
If we understand aright, this thinness
is peculiar to the later C-group, since
Classes I, II, which are not named as
late classes,[1] are described as " of fairly
thick ware," showing "a considerable
admixture of *tibn.*" [2] But when we
come to Class XI, which is stated to
belong to the later C-group period,[3]
and the shapes of which [4] correspond
with our pan-grave bowls, we find it
described as "thin polished black,
brown and red ware." [5] Hence it
appears that the thinness of the
pottery differentiates the later C-group
(i.e. the pan-grave age) from the
earlier.[6]

---

[1] *A.S.N. Bull.*, no. 6, p. 3. Cf. Reisner's description of
" thick black-topped bowls," which continue from the
B-group into the C-group, *A.S.N.*, 1907–08, p. 333, 3.

[2] *I.e.*, chopped straw; *A.S.N.*, 1908–09, p. 19, no. 1.

[3] *A.S.N. Bull.*, no. 6, p. 3, no. iii.

[4] *A.S.N.*, 1909–10, Pl. 32, b, 1–3 ; cf. our Pl. XIV, н 1,
2, 3.

[5] *A.S.N.*, 1909–10, p. 19, Class xi.

[6] Softness and thickness is said to be a characteristic of
another of the wares, the black incised, of the C-group
pottery of the pre-pan-grave age. *A.S.N.*, 1909–10,
p. 15, no. 4.

(c) *Decoration.*

The pan-graves decorate only the upper part of the bowl[1] (with only two exceptions, P., *D.P.*, Pl. xl., 36, and probably the similarly decorated vase, type H 3, Pl. XIV). The earlier C-group decorates the whole surface[2] (*A.S.N. Bull.*, no. 6, p. 4, Classes II, III, cf. *A.S.N.*, 1907–08, Pl. 61 b; *A.S.N.*, 1908–09, Pl. 39 f, Pl. 40, Pl. 46 d; *A.S.N.*, 1909–10, Pls. 29, 31, 31).

The arrangement of the hatched patterns on the pan-grave pottery is totally different from that on the great majority of the C-group pots. Though here again the late C-group in Classes XI, XII, varies from the early classes and resembles the pan-graves. A study of the great collection of potsherds published by Weigall[3] will convince the reader of the complete difference between the Nubian hatched ware and that of the pan-graves. The earlier C-group Classes II, III,[4] and many specimens in the plates of the reports are decorated all over the

---

[1] It may put a pattern on the bottom of the bowl also, P., *D.P.*, Pl. xl, 25, p. 47. The latest C-group does the same, *A.S.N.*, 1909–10, Pl. 35, d, and p. 18, fig. xi, said, on p. 3, *A.S.N. Bull.*, no. 6, to belong to the later type of C-group graves.

[2] The tendency to drop the decoration of the whole surface and to confine attention to the rim is seen at work in what is called the later C-group, which to judge by its pottery is not as late as the pan-graves. Here on some bowls (such as *A.S.N.*, 1909–10, p. 131, fig. 180; p. 133, fig. 187; p. 134, fig. 188, 1; p. 135, fig. 195, 1, &c.), the decoration has become reduced to a few lines radiating from the base to the still heavily decorated rim. Then again, on other bowls (such as p. 118, fig. 138, 5; p. 119, fig. 143. 6; p. 127, fig. 169, 4, &c.), even this decoration has disappeared, and only the strongly marked decoration of the brim is left.

[3] *Antiquities of Lower Nubia*, Pls. lxxvi to xciv; cf. also MacIver and Woolley, *Areika*, Pls. 10, 11, 12.

[4] *A.S.N. Bull.*, no. 6, p. 4.

The white filling of the incised patterns on bowls, though common in the C-group, does not occur in the pan-graves, and is not said to occur in the late C-group.[1]

The red, yellow, blue and green painted details of the C-group Class X[2] are entirely lacking in the pan-graves, and are presumably absent from the late C-group.

The ornament of impressed triangles in various groupings[3] is entirely lacking in the pan-graves, and is presumably absent from the late C-group. Perhaps its place in the pan-grave pottery is taken by the rows of pit marks at the brim (see types H 3, 4).

The coarse, smooth, red pottery bound with chopped straw[4] has never been found in the pan-graves. This ware evidently resembles the rough ware, R, of the pre-dynastic age in its clay, but not in its shapes. Its presence once more connects the C-group with, while its absence divides the pan-graves from, the pre-dynastic civilization.

The use of shells bored for suspension and otherwise by the pan-grave people connects them with the C-group people, while the much greater use made of them by the former differentiates them strongly from the latter, in whose graves such shells are comparatively rarely met with.[5] Further, in the C-group many of the ornamental shells are cowries with the backs cut off, a form not found in the pan-graves.

Yet other differences between the pan-grave and earlier C-group civilizations will be found in the—

.—

---

[1] *A.S.N..Bull.*, no. 6, pp. 3, 5.

[2] *A.S.N.*, 1909–10, pp. 15, 19, Pls. 39, 40. See also *A.S.N.*, 1908–09, Pl. 39, f, 2; WEIGALL, *Antiquities of Lower Nubia*, Frontispiece and Pl. A.

[3] *A.S.N.*, 1907–08, Pl. 61, b, 5; *A.S.N.*, 1908–09, Pl. 40, a, 2, 6, c, 3, 5, 6, Pl. 46, d, 1, 2, 3, 5; *A.S.N.*, 1909–10, Pls. 29, 30, 31, 32, c; *A.S.N. Bull.*, no. 6, Classes IA, II, III.

[4] *A.S.N.*, 1908–09, Pl. 47, and *A.S.N.*, 1909–10, p. 18, Class IV.

[5] *A S.N.*, 1907–08, p. 54, no. 183; *A.S.N.*, 1908–09, p. 56, no. 6, &c.; *A.S.N.*, 1909–10, p. 110, no. 51, p. 113. no. 8, p. 114, no. 13, &c.

[6] Out of all the C-group material now published only one possible case is reported. See *A.S.N.*, 1908–09, p. 107, no. 103.

[7] A single stone axe-head is reported by *A.S.N.*, 1909–10, p. 134, no. 412.

[8] Mats of these types are not indicated in the *A.S.N.* publications, whereas others are. For references see the next section, dealing with the classes absent from the pan-graves.

H

Absence from the pan-graves of :—

Button seals. *A.S.N.*, 1907–08, Pl. 71 a,
nos. 14, 15, 16, 36; 1908–09, Pl. 42 b,
nos. 30, 32, 33, 34, p. 160, no. 14;
1909–10, Pl. 36 e, nos. 17, 18, 20.

Finger rings. *A.S.N.*, 1908–09, p. 83,
no. 225, and often.

Model pots. *A.S.N.*, 1908–09, p. 19,
no. 1, 4, Pl. 39 e, &c.

True needles with eyes. *A.S.N.*, 1907–08,
Pl. 66 b, no. 45, 46 ?, p. 164, no. 85.

Feather fan (?). *A.S.N.*, 1907–08. p. 195,
no. 5; 1908–09, Pl. 39 c, but perhaps
early Dynastic, not C-group.

Dagger. *A.S.N.*, 1909–10, p. 17, 117,
no. 111, p. 139, no. 434.

Mirrors. *A.S.N.*, 1907–08, Pl. 65 d, 2, 3;
1908–09, Pl. 39 c; 1909–10, Pl. 37 c, 4.

Steatopygous dolls. *A.S.N.*, 1908–09,
Pl. 39 a, b; 1909–10, Pl. 37 a, d, 1, 2.

Bead cloth. *A.S.N.*, 1908–09, Pl. 39 d,
p. 81, no. 226. A piece from the
C-group at Faras is to be published
shortly by the Oxford Expédition to
Nubia.

Porphyry (?) beads. *A.S.N.*, 1907–08,
p. 161, no. 28; 1908–09, p. 85,
no. 331, Pl. 56, 6; 1909–10, Pl. 37 e,
2, and often.

Split cowries. *A.S.N.*, 1907–08, Pl. 66 e,
7; 1908–09, p. 84, no. 310, and
often.

Objects, called buttons (?). *A.S.N.*, 1907–
08, Pl. 70 b, 15; 1908–09, Pl. 37 b, 2.

Diagonally woven matting. *A.S.N.*,
1907–08, p. 164, nos. 73, 85, p. 165,
no. 86, p. 186, no. 159, p. 223,
no. 423, &c.; 1909–10, p. 17.

Mat of bound rushes. *A.S.N.*, 1907–08,
p. 267, no. 257, &c.

Among other resemblances will be found :—

Burial of animals' skulls and horns, which
are often painted. Pl. III, 1. P., *D.P.*,

[1] Not the long object under which is the figure 8, but
the small penannular ring alongside it.

Glazed cylinder beads. Type 16. *A.S.N.*,
1907–08, Pl. 70 b, 3.

Shell-strip bracelets. Pl. III, 3. *A.S.N.*,
1909–10, p. 132, no. 361, and often.

Noticeable absence of amulets, except for
a very few small ones. Pl. VIII.
A.S.N., 1907–08, p. 338, 8.[1]

Tortoise-shell bracelets. Pls. III, 2, 2,
XII, 10. *A.S.N.*, 1908–09, p. 82,
no. 419, p. 83, no. 235, &c., but types
not stated.

Sandals. Pl. IX. *A.S.N.*, 1908–09,
p. 82, no. 383, p. 83, no. 235, p. 178,
no. 102, &c., but types not stated.

Leather (occasionally dyed red). p. 26.
A.S.N., 1908–09, p. 84, no. 249, and
often.

Pierced leather work. Pls. IV, 2, X, 2.
A.S.N., 1908–09, p. 60, no. 121.

By means of the foregoing tabulation of
resemblances and differences we are able to form
some conclusion as to how intimately the pan-
graves are connected with the C-group of Nubia.
We find that even here, unmistakable as the
connection is, our intrusive pan-grave civilization
maintains its isolation, and the relationship is
not close.

It is evident that the pan-grave civilization of
Egypt is practically identical with that of the
latest phase of the C-group civilization. But
here the parallel ceases, for the divergence from
the earlier C-group is profound, and seems too
complete to allow of explanation, on the hypo-
thesis either of development or of merely
increasing poverty. We will not here include
such a change as that of the orientation of the
burials, as this seems to have occurred during
an earlier phase of the C-group age, and so may

---

[1] This, however, is difficult to reconcile with the state-
ment on p. 335, no. 8, which can only be comparative and
mean that small amulets are not unknown as in the
pan-graves.

Nubia to South Egypt, and it has been shown
(p. 44) that mingled with them were a few
representatives of a different civilization, that of
the black-topped cups with flared rims and a
grey band.

Now two of the differences between the pan-
grave and the earlier C-group peoples were
found to be the use, by the former, of woven
elephant's (?) hair and lip-studs. These suggested connections with the Sudan, while the
lip-stud also formed a link between the pan-
grave people and those of the civilization of the
black-topped cups with a grey band and flared
rim. At about the period of the pan-grave
civilization, we know there was another important civilization in the Sudan not far from the
C-group people, which is undoubtedly related to
that of the black-topped cups with a grey band
and flared rim. This is the civilization recently
brought to light at Kerma, and we already know
it to have used woven hair (giraffe's?), and to
have used small hard-stone palettes, to have
manufactured thongs of woven leather, to have
made pottery remarkable for its thinness and
quality,[1] to have used a moulding at the rim of
some of its bowls,[2] and to have given straighter
sides to many of them.[3] Here, then, we have six

---

[1] *Ä.Z.*, 1914, p. 37, nos. 9, 11, 13, 15. We are not told
what the C-group sandal was like, so we are prevented
from comparing it with the pan-grave types, which have
shown themselves to be unusual. We can, however, point
out that the very unusual arrangement requiring two holes
at the toe is found again at Kerma (*Ä.Z.*, 1914, Pl. v,
fig. 9; better, *Boston Bulletin*, no. 69, fig. 29), though
beyond this the resemblance does not go.

[2] *Boston Museum of Fine Arts Bulletin*, xii, no. 69, fig. 14.
The first bowl on the left of the third row of the top photograph and the first bowl on the left of the third row of the
lower photograph exhibit this feature.

[3] Had we cared to speculate further we might have

CHAPTER VIII.

OBJECTS FROM THE NEW KINGDOM CEMETERY.

Plates XVIII–XXV.

THE position and appearance of the New
Kingdom Cemetery have been described in
Chapter I. Unfortunately it had been so
completely worked out both by the Government
and by native plunderers that only a very small
portion was left to be excavated. From the
small area left to us it was hardly to be
expected that results of great scientific value
would be obtained. We were, however, for-
tunate in obtaining a large number of objects of
striking and unusual types, of which some
description must here be given.

Plate XVIII, no. 1, B 170. Two views of
a sandal of the ordinary New Kingdom type.
The upper view shows the surface, and the
lower shows the same sandal tilted on to its side
to show both sole and edge. In this second
photograph the sandal is so tilted that what was
the lower ankle-strap in the first picture has
become the upper in the second. The sandal is
quite different from those of the pan-graves, for
it is made by sewing together three thicknesses
of leather with very fine neat stitching. This is
well seen in the top picture, especially near the
toe. It will be noticed in the lower picture that
this fine stitchery does not pass through to the
under side of the sandal. The ankle-straps are
cut from these pieces of leather, and are bound
round with strips of red-dyed leather. After
these thicknesses have been sewn together to
form the body of the sandal, an extra sole or
clump has been sewn on with large coarse
stitches passing right through to the surface.

---

[1] See above, pp. 24 ff.

there was a niche. The long axis ran north
and south.

Plate XVIII, no. 2, B 15. The forepart of an
extremely interesting sandal, the sole of which
is made like the previous one, of three thicknesses of leather stitched together, an extra sole
or clump having been added underneath. The
guard to the ankle-strap which comes from the
clump is seen at the lower side of the sandal.
It curls up over the place whence the ankle-
strap has been broken off. The sandal was
secured by a toe-strap which passed into the
sole. The special interest, however, lies in the
fact that, in spite of this complete and usual
apparatus for fastening on the sandal, uppers
have been added, and have been laced together
with four laces. One half with the laces
remains and is quite visible in the illustration,
but although the other has entirely disappeared
its presence is suggested by the two remaining
stitches on the upper side, which fastened something now lost.

Here then we actually have the transition
from the simple sandal to the shoe, and it has
not yet been realised that with the use of
uppers the toe-strap has become superfluous as a
means of keeping on the foot-gear. Unfortunately the heel is not preserved, to show
whether the shoe was open at the back or was
closed all round, as the remains of the stitching
would rather seem to indicate. The idea of
putting on an upper no doubt arose from the
custom of broadening the strap or of inserting a
protector over the instep to prevent chafing.
This custom is as old as the first Egyptian
Dynasty, for Narmer's sandals are shown with a
very broad piece for this purpose.[1] It is to be
seen from time to time throughout the length
of Egyptian civilization, but generally in a
much less exaggerated form. It comes to a
head in the great sandals in the tomb of

[1] See fig. 7 on p. 24.

as " hair rings," but here one of them is seen in place in the lobe of the ear. It also appears to have been passed through a hole in the skin, and not to have been merely nipped on. The form of the ear is just distinguishable above it. This ring was of hard opaque white stone (chalcedony ?). In the other ear at the time of discovery there were two more specimens similarly arranged ; of these, one was of the same white stone, while the other was of carnelian.

The rest of the tomb-group (Pl. XXV) was interesting. No. 56 is a large portion of a figure vase in the form of a bird. It was made of a fine quality W and D[1] clay, as was the Decorated pottery of the middle pre-dynastic age. As in the latter, the decoration has been put on with red paint. This specimen had been fired sufficiently for the surface to begin to turn slightly yellow or white. Bird vases are most common in Egypt in the pre-dynastic age.[2] Bird vases, along with others in animal form, are quite common in the second period (early bronze (copper ?) age) at Susa (DE MORGAN, *Délégation en Perse*, xiii, Pls. xxx, 9, xxxvii, 1, 2, 7, xxxviii, 2, 11, 12). Several are known from Tell-el-Mutesellim in North Palestine.[3] A duck vase, similar to that from Tell-el-Mutesellim, in blue faience, comes from Cyprus.[4] The subject will be found more fully treated on p. 56.

---

[1] The term W and D ware is used throughout this article for the hard close pink ware with white specks in it, which is so regularly used for the Wavy-handled and Decorated classes of pre-dynastic pottery. It is practically the same material as the *ballás* and the *qulleh* of modern Egypt, but is generally only fired to a pink colour, whereas the modern examples being fully fired become greenish, or yellowish white. Therefore the expression W and D ware gives a better idea of the appearance than either the name *ballás* or *qulleh* ware. However, when this same ware is sufficiently fired to look like the modern representatives, we use the name *qulleh*.

[2] Miss MURRAY, *Historical Studies*, Pls. xxii, xxiii.

[3] SCHUMACHER, *Tell el Mutesellim*, p. 89, Abb. 131, a, b, p. 90, Abb. 132.

[4] MURRAY, *Excavations in Cyprus*, p. 115, fig. 166, no. 5.

No. 58 is the neck of a bottle of fine thin [1]
W and D ware, pink in colour and turning
slightly white on the outside. The lip had been
pinched into four angles.

No. 59 is one of the little Syrian jugs of
black polished pottery. The burnishing marks
run up and down the sides, not round and
round. It had contained ointment, and when
first discovered the jug smelt not unlike the
ointment of the pre- and proto-dynastic and
pan-grave times. The ointment, moreover, had
cracked the vessel, as it so often cracked the
earlier receptacles.

The tomb was a pit $2 \cdot 50 \times 0 \cdot 80$ m. and $1 \cdot 60$ m.
deep. The long axis was north and south.
There were no chambers, but merely a niche on
the west side about $0 \cdot 60$ m. wide $\times 0 \cdot 80$ m.
high.

Plate XIX, no. 3. Group B 154. For the rest
of the pottery see Pl. XXV. This group is only
of interest for the pottery doll. The alabaster
kohl-pot on the left, having lost its cover, had
been provided with a new one of bright blue
glaze. The two pots on the upper row are of
the usual W and D ware, and are decorated in
dark red. On Pl. XXV, pots 54, 55 were of
similar ware, while nos. 52, 53 were painted red,
but not polished.

Plate XX, see also Pl. XXIII. Group B 101.
The most striking object is a vase in the form of
a woman holding a lute. She wears only a
girdle, and in the back view the hair is seen to
be drawn back to a plaited pigtail, which forms
the handle. The vase is made of alabaster, and
that the workmanship is Egyptian is sufficiently
evidenced by the treatment of the eyes and
mouth. Nevertheless, the idea is foreign, and is
no doubt connected with the zoomorphic art of
Western Asia, and with the Greek rhytons. The
Egyptian specimens have a neck with slightly
concave sides rising from the head. Similar
necks occur on such figure vases of Greek

[1] Cf. BIRCH, Ancient Pottery, 1873, fig. 120.

[2] See LAYARD, Nineveh and its Remains, ii, pp. 303, 304 ;
BIRCH, Ancient Pottery, 1873, fig. 146.

[3] Published in Historical Studies, pp. 40–46, and Pls.
xii, xxv.

[4] SEAGER, Explorations in the Island of Mochlos, figs.
32, xiii, g, and 34.

[5] HAWES, Gournia, x, 11.

[6] MACALISTER, The Exploration of Gezer, i, p. 306, fig. 162.

no. 6. It is a very blundered and imperfect attempt at the VIth Chapter of the Book of the Dead, which is commonly written on such figures. On the left side are faience pendants, on the right side beads of a reddish coloured resin. The finger rings are shown in the top row, of which the second from the left, representing a uraeus, should be noticed. There is also an *uzat* eye, several penannular ear-rings, and a scarab. The design on the base of this will be found on Pl. XXIII, no. 10.

On this plate are also the pots. The large one, no. 7, was painted white on the outside and was decorated with blue and red bands. Another of similar shape had turned white in patches during the firing. Both contained ashes of vegetable material, apparently largely *halfa*-grass, just like the pre-dynastic ash burials. No. 8 was red-painted and whitewashed, and two others like it were merely red-painted, as was no. 9. No. 11 is of *qulleh* ware. No. 12 belongs to a very distinct class, of which nos. 33, 34 on Pl. XXIV are further examples. There were only four general types of this class, all of them deep wide-mouthed vessels, of which the great majority approximated to nos. 12, 33. The class was made of the hard red ware, but of an exceptionally fine smooth quality, which had a tendency to turn white in the firing. It was regularly painted red all over the upper part of the vase, as indicated in the drawings. The two splashes of paint on no. 12 show that during the process of painting the pot was spinning clockwise. Thus the wheel was probably turned by the potter's right hand. The large pan, no. 13, has been supported by a cord while drying, as is still done to-day.

This group came from a large pit 4·00 × 2·30 m. and 4·00 m. deep. The long axis was north and south, and at a depth of 2·30 m. were two small chambers and two niches. The chambers were at the north and south ends, while the niches were at the east and west sides. They were all quite empty. Lower still, at the depth of 4·00 m., there was a single chamber at the south end. It was 2·40 × 2·20 m. in size and 1·00 m. high. It had been bricked up, and the objects here shown were found just inside the bricking. There had been five burials, in painted and inscribed wooden coffins, which had fallen to pieces.

---

[1] P., *N.B.*, Pl. vii, 1, p. 35.

turned green on the outside, with a patch of red
showing occasionally. They have a beautiful
smooth silky surface, not unlike that of some of
the pre- and proto-dynastic cylinder jars in
texture. One of the smaller ones still had
remains of ointment inside, and was cracked, as
ointment vessels so often are. A great quantity
of pottery came to light, for which see Pl. XXIV,
mostly of the usual style. One example of
no. 25 was whitewashed, as was the rim of
no. 36. The rims of the other two examples
of no. 25 were painted red. Nos. 33, 34 have
already been treated on p. 57. There were four
specimens of no. 33. Nos. 48, 49, 50 were all
of the ordinary hard brown ware of the period
and unpainted, but while no. 48 was very rough,
nos. 49, 50 were finely made and thin. The
common type of mouth in these last two, without a neck or even a rim, although the sides
incurve as if to receive one, is as ancient as the
pre-dynastic period.[1] In this group there were
three examples of no. 50. No. 51 is of *qulleh*
ware.

The tomb consisted of a shaft 2·60 × 2·00 m.
and 4·30 m. deep. It contained two storeys
of chambers at the N. and S. ends of the
shaft. Those at a depth of 3·20 m. had been
emptied. At a depth of 4·30 m., at the S.
end, was a small niche which had been walled
up. It had contained a burial in a wooden
painted anthropomorphic coffin. No objects
were found here. Opposite it, at the N. end,
was a large chamber 5·00 × 2·60 m. and
1·20 m. high. It had been walled up, and had
contained fifteen interments in painted wood
and stucco coffins similar to the previous one.
It was from here that the objects were collected.

Plate XXI, no. 2, see also Plate XXV. Group
B 36. The central piece shows the upper part of
a female figure vase. It is made of the ordinary
hard red clay of the period. It never possessed

---

[1] See P., *N.B.*, Pl. xxi, 75 a, xxii, 27.

Plate XXII, no. 1, see also Plate XXV.
Group B 90. This contained a plaque about
150 mm. long, of a very poor quality blue glaze.

A side view of it is numbered 67 on Pl. XXV, where it will be seen to be grooved. This groove runs round all four edges. Both surfaces are slightly convex, and both are glazed. Though this is hardly suitable for a tile for inlaying on a wall, yet the object can hardly be anything else. Thus the grooves on the edges would be for the purpose of fixing in the cement. If so, this system is quite different from that of the early period of the Ist and IIIrd Dynasties, where the central part of the back projects, is slightly undercut, and is bored through to receive a wire.[1] It is also different from the usual New Kingdom method, where the plaques are flat at the back without projections, grooves, or other means of fastening.[2] Inlaying with tiles was not uncommon in the New Kingdom. Beside it are a pair of small toggles(?) of ivory. Though only one is bored at each end, both have a deep notch or open hole at one end. It may only be that in the boring a piece broke out. Only these two were found. Similar objects, but bored at both ends, are known in the VIth Dynasty;[3] and a number of others of the intermediate period between the XIIth and XVIIIth Dynasties, from grave Y 16 of Diospolis Parva, are now in the bead-cases of the Edwards Collection. Another, but larger, of

Plate XXII, no. 2, see also Plate XXV. Group B 157. This group shows a bronze implement of a type generally taken to be a razor. In B 81 another of similar shape was found, but this had had a handle projecting from the side. With it, in the northern chamber, were found the two alabaster dishes. From the southern chamber came the scarab of a dark greyish blue glaze, and the alabaster ear-stud. From this chamber also came some fine blue and a few small red jasper disc beads, also a little gold foil. The back of the scarab is shown in Pl. XXV, no. 68. On this plate is also shown the pottery, nos. 69 to 80; and to this should be added the small

---

[1] PETRIE, Abydos, ii, Pl. viii, 181, 182; BORCHARDT, Ä.Z., xxx, Pl. 1.

[2] As for instance in the well-known tiles of Rameses III from Tell el Yahudiyeh; BRUGSCH, Rec. de Trav., viii, Pl. i, figs. 1, 2. Small tiles for inlay are not at all uncommon in the New Kingdom in the time of Akhenaton (PETRIE, Tell el Amarna, Pls. vi, xviii–xx), Seti I (PETRIE, Palace of Apries, Pl. xxii, no. 3, p. 15), and Merenptah (op. cit., Pl. xxii, nos. 1, 2, and p. 15). At this time inlay of alabaster is used, see Pl. xxii, no. 14, and p. 15. Another tile of this king, or of Seti II, comes from Khata'neh, and others of Seti II (GRIFFITH, Tell el Yahudiyeh, p. 57, Pl. xix, fig. 28). Of Rameses III, besides those from Tell el Yahudiyeh, others are known from Medinet Habu (DARESSY, Annales du Service, xi, pp. 49 ff, Pls. i to iv). To the tiles of early times may be added those named by Maspero as bearing the cartouche of Pepi I (Les Origines, 243, note 1).

[3] P., C.A., i, Pl. vii, E 45.

[4] A.S.N., 1908–09, Pl. 37, b, no. 19.

[5] We are indebted to the authorities of the Natural History Museum of South Kensington for the names.

rough pot with rudimentary handles which has
been photographed. This group produced a
remarkable number and variety of the small
tubular pots. Of no. 69, which was red polished,
there were twenty-one specimens. Of no. 73,
which was red painted, there were three
specimens, and four of no. 74, all of which
were made of a coarse *qulleh* ware. Two vases,
nos. 71, 72, were red-polished with a black-
painted rim, which fashion does not come in
until the XVIIIth Dynasty. The idea may

CHAPTER IX.

FOREIGN POTTERY OF THE NEW KINGDOM.

THE New Kingdom Cemetery yielded an unusually large proportion of foreign pottery of various types. Egyptologists as a whole have adopted a somewhat uncritical attitude in dealing with these un-Egyptian products, and have shown too great a readiness to assign certain types of vase to the Ægean, to Cyprus, or to Syria, without even asking whether such types occur in these regions, still less whether they are native there.

Difficulties and misunderstandings could easily be cleared away if excavators who find foreign vases in Egypt would make a careful examination and record of the nature of the clay and even the smallest details of technique, and if, in making comparisons with other countries, they would keep the question of date continually before their eyes. If this were done, we should less often be confronted with the ludicrous spectacle of an Egyptian archaeologist and a Palestinian each explaining one and the same type of vase found in his area as an import from that of the other.

With these considerations in mind we have attempted the following full analysis of the foreign forms found at Balabish.

1. The *bilbils*. Pl. XXV, no. 79 is made of a soft reddish brown clay and is burnished brown on the outside. This is one of the regular materials for *bilbils* in Egypt, though still more frequently they are made of a blackish grey ware, thin, hard and brittle, and breaking in a flaky manner. A specimen made of this ware was found in B 173. These vessels are burnished black and often have a metallic lustre.

in Egypt[1] is not figured from Cyprus. The only
type which is found equally in both lands seems
to be the scarce double vase.[2] Yet in this
island the technique of making parts separately,
and thrusting them into the partly dried body,
is observed in other classes of vessels which also
have a neck and handle.

This class is generally thought to be native to
the Syrian coastland, and Myres has suggested
that some of it may have been made in Cyprus.[3]

2. The spindle-shaped bottle, Pl. XXV,
no. 81, though well known, is always a rare
type. It is made of a very hard, pure, brownish
red clay, and is polished a light yellow-red, no
doubt acquired by means of haematite. Bottles
something like this shape and painted red are
brought by the Syrians in the Menkheperresenb
fresco,[4] and a similar type is brought by the
Keftiuans in that of Rekhmire.[4] There are
several from Bronze Age Cyprus,[5] but they are
probably not of Cypriote manufacture.[6] One
now in the Ashmolean Museum is said to have
been found on the island of Melos, but none are
figured from Phylakopi in this island. A single
one is figured among L.M. I pottery from Gournia
in Crete.[7] None come from Tell el Mutesellim or
Ta'annek in North Palestine, or from Jericho,

---

[1] As for instance P., *H.I.C.*, Pl. xii c, figs. 23, 24.

[2] P., *H.I.C.*, Pl. xii B, right-hand bottom corner, or P., *L.G.M.*, Pl. xxi. Compare these with MYRES and RICHTER, *Catalogue of the Cyprus Museum*, Pl. ii, 252 ; MYRES, *Handbook of the Cesnola Collection*, pp. 40, 358 ; MURRAY, *Excavations in Cyprus*, p. 45, fig. 71, no. 953.

[3] MYRES, *op. cit.*, p. 37.

[4] *L.A.A.A.*, 1913, Pl. ix, 13, Pl. xi, 65, x, 40.

[5] MURRAY, *op. cit.*, figs. 66, 74. MYRES and RICHTER, *op. cit.*, no. 300, p. 47 and Pl. ii. MYRES, *op. cit.*, nos. 369 to 375, p. 41, where they are said to be probably not of Cypriote manufacture.

[6] The curious vessel, no. 1108, p. 40, fig. 68, MURRAY, *op. cit.*, which is like an arm holding a cup, is burnished with the same rather unusual yellow-red colour that is usual on the spindle-shaped bottles. It is now in the British Museum.

[7] HAWES, *Gournia*, Pl. viii, 25.

[8] PETRIE, *Tell el Hesy*, Pl. vii, 121, but it is included with light brown *porous* pottery, p. 44.

[9] MACALISTER, *op. cit.*, ii, p. 177, fig. 338.

[10] TAYLOR, *Alphabet*, ii, p. 123.

[11] EDGAR and others, *Phylakopi*, p. 179, fig. F, 13.

[12] MYRES, *op. cit.*, p. 41.

[13] P., *I.K.G.*, Pl. xv, col. 5 and p. 11.

[14] Cf. WOOLLEY, *L.A.A.A.*, vi, Pls. xix, xxvi.

[15] SELLIN, *Tell Ta'annek*, Pl. v, fig. a.

[16] SCHUMACHER, *Tell el Mutesellim*, p. 70, fig. 90 i, p. 81 and p. 82, fig. 111.

known from South Palestine, chiefly at Gezer and Lachish, but also at Jericho;[1] it is also known from Cyprus. It does not seem to be native to any of these countries, and appears in each of them about the same time, but later in Cyprus than in the others. For the pilgrim-flask proper, of a flat shape with two small handles, hardly[2] seems to enter the island until some time after it is found in Egypt and Palestine, i.e. not until the Early Iron Age, from 1200 B.C. onwards.[3] It is found in Egypt in the XVIIIth Dynasty, and at Gezer it is introduced in the second Semitic period,[4] which lasts until the end of the same dynasty. At Gezer it becomes more common later,[5] while at Lachish it does not occur until the later period, i.e. from 900 to 700 B.C.[6] Thus, occurring as it does in Egypt just at the period of her greatest expansion in the XVIIIth and XIXth Dynasties, this foreign type is known there earlier than in Cyprus, and at about the same time as it first appears in South Palestine. Here the resemblance ceases, for such vessels of foreign manufacture are not found at a later date in Egypt, whereas it is precisely at the later period that they reach their zenith in Palestine and Cyprus. A flattened form, but of a very different vessel, is known in Cyprus still earlier in the Middle Bronze Age,[7] while the true flattened circular shape is known in the next period or Late Bronze Age,

---

[1] Sellin and Watzinger, *Jericho*, Bl. 29, c, 23, 39, E. 4b.

[2] We only find one instance of a true pilgrim-flask in the Bronze Age in Cyprus, see Murray, *op. cit.*, p. 40, fig. 68, no. 1111.

[3] Myres and Richter, *op. cit.*, pp. 21, 66, Class B, cf. Myres, *op. cit.*, p. 70, nos. 544 to 546 and p. 54.

[4] In the first Semitic period, which ended with the XIIth Dynasty, small vessels with little handles at the neck are found at Gezer. They, however, are not lentoid in shape, but globular. Macalister, *op. cit.*, ii, 142, q, iii, Pl. cxliii, figs. 3–8.

[5] Macalister, *op. cit.*, ii, 162 (j), 199 (j).

[6] Petrie, *Tell el Hesy*, p. 46.

[7] Myres, *op. cit.*, p. 24, nos. 159, 160.

[8] Myres, *op. cit.*, figs. 328, 377.

[9] As for instance, P., *H.I.C.*, Pl. xii, c, 24.

[10] Ἐφ. Ἀρχ., 1891, Pl. iii, 1; cf. for ornamentation Myres, *op. cit.*, p. 81, figs. 647, 649, &c.

[11] H. Schmidt, *Schliemann's Sammlung*, nos. 630–632 p. 34.

[12] *Op. cit.*, nos. 634 (which has a narrow neck), 635, 636.

in these, but from the side, as in the pilgrim-
flasks. The neck is long, as in the Cypriote
bottles, but not narrow, and is cut out behind
into a spout.

In Palestine the pilgrim-flask takes on a
curious form, for it acquires a spoon-shaped
mouth.[1] This type, though very rare, is said to
be not unknown in Cyprus.[2]

One pilgrim-flask is figured as being of
Assyrian origin,[3] and hence is probably much
later than the Egyptian specimens, and contemporary with those of Cyprus, Lachish, and the
later period at Gezer. Thus the form suddenly
extends widely over the eastern Levant, and all
that can be said of its place of origin is that it is
probably not Cyprus, where it is found later
than in Egypt or Gezer. Possibly the fact of a
bottle of this shape being made of the rare metal
tin[4] will give a clue as to the home of the type.

The flattened shape and small handles on the
shoulder of the pilgrim-flasks are as old as the
Middle Pre-dynastic Age.[5] This age, like the
XVIIIth Dynasty, shows many connections with
Asia, of which it will be sufficient to mention

---

[1] MACALISTER, *op. cit.*, iii, Pls. lxv, 25, lxxxvii, 8 ;
cf. Pl. lxxxviii, 6, and SELLIN and WATZINGER, *Jericho*,
Bl. 39, E, 4, b, and perhaps SCHUMACHER, *Tell el Mutesellim*,
p. 82, fig. 111. In most of these spoon-mouthed flasks
the handles have been turned at right angles to the neck,
no doubt to accommodate the broad mouth. For the
addition of a vessel at the mouth of a vase in which to
receive the liquid, compare the red-polished vessel from
Cyprus, no. 1108, already referred to in note 62, p. 6.

[2] MYRES, quoted by MACALISTER in *Gezer*, ii, p. 179, k.

[3] BIRCH, *Ancient Pottery*, fig. 77.

[4] AYRTON and others, *Abydos*, iii, Pl. xvii, 20, p. 50.

[5] P., *N.B.*, Pl. xii, 72, and also 71, now in the Ashmolean
Museum, numbered 1895, 213 ; MACIVER and MACE, *El
Amrah and Abydos*, Pl. xvi, fig. 9 ; QUIBELL, *Hierakonpolis*, ii, Pl. xxx, figs. 3, 4, where the handles are bored in
the opposite direction. The wide neck and very small
handles somewhat removed from it are seen again in the
New Kingdom, PETRIE, *Qurneh*, Pl. xlii, fig. 942, cf. fig. 757,
p. 13 ; or the wide neck in conjunction with the more usual
handles at this period, ENGELBACH, *Riqqeh and Memphis VI*,
Pl. xiv, S, 40. For the flattened shape without the little
handles, see P., *L.G.M.*, Pl. xi, 32, a–f.

[6] P., *I.K.G.*, Pl. xvii, 9, p. 17, dated to Amenhotep III ;
Pl. xviii, 61, p. 18, dated to Rameses II ; Pl. xix, 14, p. 18,
dated to Seti II.

[7] P., *H.I.C.*, Pl. xxi.

[8] *Op. cit.*, Pl. xxi, 1, 4.

[9] *Op. cit.*, Pl. xii c, 24.

[10] GARSTANG, *El Arabah*, Pl. xxi, E 158, 233 ; MACIVER
and MACE, *El Amrah and Abydos*, Pl. xliv, D 16 B ; cf. l, D 17.

base-ring added.[1] This would seem to be a
development from the more simple type of
which our vase is a specimen. Thus, like the
true pilgrim-flask of flattened form, it does
not seem to have entered Cyprus until an age
later than that at which it was known in other
countries.

In B 38 we found the neck and shoulders of a
similar vase, but of a circular not flattened form.[2]
It was made of the same hard, pure, buff clay,
but in the outer portions of the walls it had
turned slightly redder. It thus forms a con-
necting link between the buff clay of no. 83 and
the similar but red clay of the spindle-shaped
bottle no. 81. In this case the neck has been
moulded up out of the body itself, and has not
been made separately and thrust into the semi-
dry clay of the body. Unlike no. 83 this vase
was decorated with bands running round hori-
zontally. The bands are in a dully polished red
paint, and just enough remains to show that
they consisted of narrow lines between broad
ones, a decoration similar to that of no. 84.

Pl. XXIII, nos. 3, 4, are made of a red W
and D ware fairly thin, and are polished red on
the outside. No. 3 still contained remains of
ointment. We were able to see that the neck
of one example of no. 46 had been thrust
through the partly dry clay of the body.

4. False-necked amphorae, stirrup-handled
vases or Bügelkannen, Pl. XXV, 84–87. The

---

[1] See MYRES, *op. cit.*, p. 49, figs. 445, 446. This latter
type, with the base-ring added, though still far from
common there, occurs in the Aegean area more than does
the true pilgrim-flask. A single specimen is recorded from
Knossos (EVANS, *Prehistoric Tombs of Knossos* (Archaeologia, lix), p. 123, fig. 117, no. 76, E). Another is figured
from Crete or Cyprus (FURTWAENGLER and LOESCHKE,
Mykenische Vasen, Pl. xiv, 92), and yet another from
Boeotia (*op. cit.*, Pl. xx, fig. 149). A similar form, but
with one handle only, is figured as no. 145 on the same
plate.

[2] It must have been a bottle like MURRAY, *op. cit.*, p. 34,
fig. 62, no. 1222, or MACIVER and WOOLLEY, *Buhen*, Pl. 48,
S, xlii.

K

The Minoans in the Senmut fresco do not bring any vases of this type, nor do the Syrians or Keftiuans, unless two vases there depicted can be supposed to represent abnormally tall examples.[1]

No. 84 is painted in lustrous black colour with a tendency to turn red. It had five concentric circles under the base.

No. 85 was decorated with dull red paint, and had three concentric circles under the base.

No. 86 was also decorated with dull red paint, but had no circles under the base. The spout had been thrust through the semi-dry clay as in the *bilbils* (no. 79), and as in one of the pilgrim-flasks, no. 46. No. 86 contained a thick blackish brown sediment, coating the whole of the inside, presumably the remains of a liquid ointment or oil.

No. 87 was painted with dull red bands, and had no circles under the base. As the clay differed from that of the rest, and approximated to the Egyptian W and D ware, it may be that this is an Egyptian imitation of the foreign class. The Egyptians were certainly accustomed to imitate such foreign vases, for a false-necked amphora in green glaze is actually reported from the old Bulaq Museum,[2] and others in the same material, and with Egyptian decorations, are published,[3] which are evidently designed after some such foreign type. Mention has already been made of the Egyptian imitations of pilgrim-flasks in glaze. Vase no. 87 contained scented ointment similar to that of the pre- and proto-dynastic ages and of the pan-graves.

5. Plate XXV, no. 59 is of black polished pottery. It contained ointment with a sweet scent similar to that of the pre- and proto-dynastic ages and of the pan-graves. This had cracked the jug as it so often does. Small jugs

The whole of the foregoing group is quite un-Egyptian in all its shapes, and half of the vases at any rate, nos. 79, 81, 83, 84, 85, 86, are importations, clearly made of foreign clay. The others might be Egyptian imitations of foreign types. There are points of connection between the various members of the group, in that the clay of the pilgrim-flask no. 83 is identical with that of a broken fragment of a false-necked amphora, painted with lustrous blackish-red colour, which was also found at Balabish, but is not figured here. The clay of both is the same as the clay of the globular vase from B 38, to which we have recently referred (on p. 65), but in B 38 the external portion of the walls has turned pinker. All these clays are similar in texture to the redder clay of the spindle-shaped bottle no. 81. The difference in

---

[1] *L.A.A.A.*, vi, Pls. xiii, 81, xiv, 9, pp. 56, 57.

[2] GRIFFITH, *Tell el Yahudiyeh*, p. 46, no. 15.

[3] P., *I.K.G.*, Pl. xx, 1.

[4] P., *H.I.C.*, Pl. viii B, figs. 103, 106, 107, 108.

[5] Ashmolean Museum no. E 2001 is from Beni Hasan, and therefore probably of XIIth Dynasty date; and in the same museum is another from Harageh, accompanied by its label from the British School of Archaeology, which states it to date to the XIIIth Dynasty (?).

[6] None are figured from the Ægean in FURTWAENGLER and LOESCHKE, *op. cit.*, or in HAWES, *Gournia*, or in EDGAR and others, *Phylakopi*. Nor yet is it figured from Cyprus, either in MYRES and RICHTER, *op. cit.*, or in MYRES, *op. cit.*, or in MURRAY, *op. cit.* Neither is any figured from North Syria in *L.A.A.A.*, vi, Pls. xix, xxii, xxiii, xxv, xxvi.

colour might be accounted for by supposing a more complete firing in the case of the latter, as the change from buff to red had begun to take place in the vase from B 38. Moreover, all these clays, though different, are not very unlike those of the false-necked amphorae nos. 84, 85, 86.

Again the base-ring (hollow foot) is very common among those which have bases, for all the *bilbils* have either it, like no. 79, or else the allied form of a trumpet-shaped foot, which is also hollow. No. 81 is made with a base-ring, as are the false-necked amphorae nos. 84 to 87. Only the black-polished jug, no. 59, stands out. The base-ring, hollow as it is underneath, is found again very commonly in the button-foot of the black ware jugs with punctured patterns filled in with white (Tell el Yahudiyeh ware), which are found in Egypt from the XIIIth Dynasty on to Hyksos times. This ware also is of foreign origin, and is usually considered to be Syrian, though similar vases from Gezer are said to be imported from Egypt![1] On Egyptian-made vessels we believe the base-ring to be practically confined to a portion of that class of New Kingdom pottery which is Syrianizing both in shape and decoration.[2] Besides being

---

[1] MACALISTER, *op. cit.*, ii, pp. 156, 160, 161, Pl. cliii, figs. 8, 9, 10.

[2] P., *C.A.* iii, Pl. v, 33. P., *G.R.*, Pl. xxvii, F, 158, 159. Compare their wide necks and strong rims surmounting a more or less globular body with WOOLLEY, *L.A.A.A.*, vi, Pl. xxii, no. 1, which an inspection of the original shows to have the ring-base. The shape of the vase no. 6$\frac{3}{4}$ of *El Amrah and Abydos*, Pl. lv, is actually closer, but unfortunately the hollowness of the foot, which will probably be there, is not indicated. Specimens considerably closer to the Egyptian vases can be found among the North Syrian pottery that is still unpublished. Apart from these Syrianizing forms, a base-ring is quite unusual and extremely rare on Egyptian vessels, but still is not absolutely unknown. See DE MORGAN, *Tombeau Royale de Negadah*, p. 184, fig. 664; *Medum*, Pl. xxx, 17; *Mahâsna and Bêt Khallâf*, Pl. xxxv, 12; BORCHARDT, *Grabdenkmal des Königs Saḥu-reʿ*, p. 115, fig. 148, two cylinder vases, p. 116, fig. 153, one bowl, p. 117, fig. 160; P., *K.G.H.*, Pl. xvii, 7; *Abydos*, iii, Pl. xlvii, 65. This completes the

Egypt by the Syrians.[1] The same feature is seen on the lotus vases of this period, whether of faience[2] or of alabaster, such as the strange specimens from Sinai now in the Ashmolean Museum. Although it might have been thought that these would have been purely Egyptian, yet besides having the hollowed trumpet-foot, they are also shown as being brought by the Syrians and Keftiuans.[3] We content ourselves with quoting these classes, actual examples of which have been found, but a glance at the tribute scenes will emphasize the extent to which such a foot or stand was used for every kind of vase by the Syrians. The Syrianizing globular vases with the wide neck, and copies of the Syrian *bilbils* as well, are also made of glass,[4] a substance not known in Egypt before the XVIIIth Dynasty, when so many Syrian influences were at work. Both the hollow base-ring and the hollow trumpet-foot are actually found very commonly on the pottery of this age and earlier from North Syria,[5] also in Palestine,[6]

where they continue into Jewish times.[7] Both the base-ring, the button-foot, and the high trumpet-foot, all of them inadequate to their vases, are quite common in the first division of the pre-Mycenaean settlements at Troy. They are therefore much earlier than the "Syrian" or Syrianizing vessels of the Egyptian New Kingdom.s Thus the base-ring and the hollow trumpet-foot, often of inadequate dimensions, are closely connected with the vase forms of Syria and of early Troy.

Apart from these Syrianizing examples the hollow trumpet-foot is very rare in Egypt,[9] and

---

[1] In Rekhmire, see VIREY, *Mems. Miss. Franc.*, v, 1, Pl. vii, second row of deposited presents ; cf. also the vase in HALL, *Ancient History of the Near East*, Pl. xv. 1, bottom left-hand corner, where the neck is exaggerated. The type more often has handles added, as those brought by the Keftiuans in Rekhmire, in Pl. v, bottom row of deposited presents, and the vase carried by the fourth man in the top row ; also by the Syrians, as in Menkheperresenb, MÜLLER, *Egyptological Researches*, ii, Pl. 5, and more decoratively treated in Pls. 4, 6 ; cf. that brought by the Keftiuans and North Syrians on Pl. 2, and Rekhmire, top row but one of the deposited presents.

[2] P., *I.K.G.*, Pl. xvii, 8, *Meydum and Memphis III*, Pl. xxviii, 134, both now in the Ashmolean Museum, where they were examined.

[3] MÜLLER, *Egyptological Researches*, ii, Pls. 3, 5 ; cf. the second vessel from the right on Pl. 6, which, ending as it does in a sort of calix, may represent a similar idea.

[4] PETRIE, *Arts and Crafts of Ancient Egypt*, figs. 120, 121. Fig. 120 has had handles of yet another sort added.

[5] As for instance on vases similar to *L.A.A.A.*, vi, Pl. xix, *a*, and on the vases figured in the same publication on Pls. xix, *b*, 3, xxii, 1, 2, 3, 6, and many others. The vessels of Pl. xix, *a*, *b*, date to the First Bronze Period, and are therefore earlier than the XVIIIth Dynasty.

[6] MACALISTER, *op. cit.* For the high foot see Pls. xliv, 11, lxxiv, 1, lxxxi, 1, 2, 6, lxxxii, 11, lxxxiv, 7, lxxxviii, 1,

xc, 1, 2, 3, xci, 12–17, cliv, 14. For the base-ring see Pls. cliv, 11, 12, 25, clii, 17, cxxii, 14, 17, &c. See also BLISS and MACALISTER, *Excavations in Palestine*, Pl. 35, figs. 1–9, Pl. 34, figs. 1 s, 5 z, 9 s, &c. These can also be found at the other Palestinian sites of Jericho, Tell el Mutesellim, Tell Ta'annek.

[7] For the high foot in Jewish times, see *Excavations in Palestine*, Pl. 52, figs. 1, 2, Pl. 53, fig. 1 J.

[8] H. SCHMIDT, *Trojanische Altertümer*, nos. 413, 415, 448, 501, 537, 659, 667, 691–700, &c. Often the vase itself, instead of being merely flattened, is actually hollowed out underneath. See nos. 739–741, 751, &c.

[9] We only know it in connection with the plate-like tables of offering made of alabaster, which belong to the proto-dynastic period (as GARSTANG, *Mahâsna and Bêt Khallâf*, xxix), and the pottery dishes, which latter in all ages are often provided with a high stand (as for instance ENGELBACH, *Riqqeh and Memphis VI*, Pl. xxxiii, 90 b, 1, q, s, x). The frequency with which this occurs leads one to suppose that the stand does not merely represent the common Egyptian ring-stand ; for, apart from these possible exceptions, the Egyptians never fastened their ring-stands to the vessels, but kept the two separate throughout the course of their long civilization. Now on turning once more to North Syria we find published two dishes on high stands, though it is not apparent whether these are hollow or not (*L.A.A.A.*, vi, Pl. xix, *a*). These are early, being of the first Bronze Period. On expanding the search from this centre it is found that both to the East and West— in Susa (DE MORGAN, *Délégation en Perse*, xiii, p. 31, Pls. xi, 4, xii, 1), Thessaly (WACE and THOMPSON, *Prehistoric Thessaly*, "fruit-stands," pp. 16, 17, 22, types B 3, β, γ, ε, belonging to the Second Neolithic Period, and pp. 20, 112, 114, 237, type Γ 3 ξ, belonging to the end of the Neolithic and beginning of the Chalcolithic Age), and Moldavia (*Idem*, p. 257)—dishes mounted on fixed stands occur in the Neolithic and Chalcolithic periods. It there-

as a regular feature is only known to us on the stand vases of tubular or globular shape of the early pre-dynastic age.[1]

Besides the connections already observed between different members of our group of foreign vases, a large number of them contained ointment; that is to say, five pilgrim-flasks,

---

fore seems as if these Egyptian dishes do not prove to be an exception, but themselves belong to a very characteristic, widespread, and early northern type.

[1] Such as P., *N.B.*, Pl. ix, 58, 61, 65, 72, &c. Can it be, then, that these stand vases of the intrusive Early Pre-dynastic civilization are in some way connected with Syria?

---

[2] See above, pp. 14 ff.

APPENDIX

PRESENT LOCATION OF THE OBJECTS FOUND AT BALABISH.

N.B.—The number is that of the tomb in which objects were found. Where no details are given it is to be understood that all the objects from the tomb in question are to be found in the Museum.

UNIVERSITY OF PENNSYLVANIA, PHILADELPHIA.

226, except some of the leather and one pottery vase.

101, all except the pottery and marbles.

228, large situla vase only.

212, all except the shells.

38, 126, 209, 225.

Also samples of leather-work, and a bag of giraffe's or elephant's hair.

BROOKLYN INSTITUTE OF ARTS AND SCIENCES, BROOKLYN, N.Y.

34, vase, knife-blade and shell bracelet.

115, beads and amulets.

128, beads and amulets.

180, all except the leather.

86, 54, 90, 119, 144, 220, 231, 239, 243.

Also large bowl of black-topped pottery, and divining horn and stones.

CINCINNATI MUSEUM, CINCINNATI, OHIO.

157, pottery only.

50, 75, 181.

WELLESLEY COLLEGE, WELLESLEY, MASS.

39, except one *ushabti.*

107, less two situla vases.

129, vase with handle, and ivory gaming reeds.

153, less beads and one black-topped vase.

212, shells only.

15, 51, 58, 60, 93, 94, 103, 108, 113, 117, 131, 141, 150, 162, 182, 212, 221, 230, 233, 235, 241.

LOUISVILLE MUSEUM, LOUISVILLE, KENTUCKY.

16, 111.

UNIVERSITY OF ILLINOIS, UBANA, ILLINOIS.

134, 152.

CORNELL UNIVERSITY MUSEUM, ITHACA, N.Y.

101, pottery and marbles only.
128, carnelian necklace and amulets.
180, fragments of leather.
213, portion of pierced leather apron.
226, fragments of leather.
227, beads only.
23, 49, 64, 154.
Also set of divining pebbles and bone hair ornaments.

INDEX.

INDEX.

PLATES.

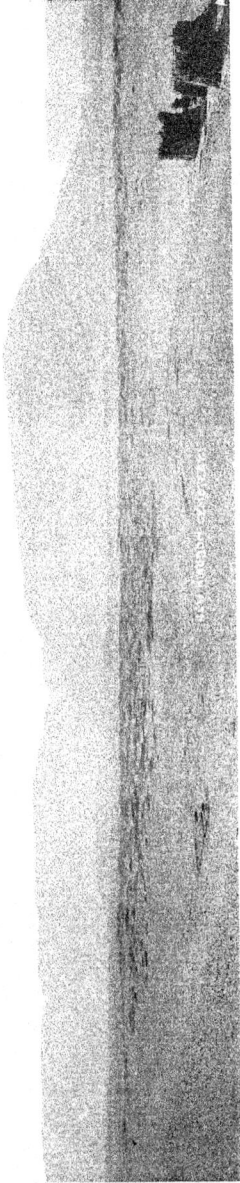

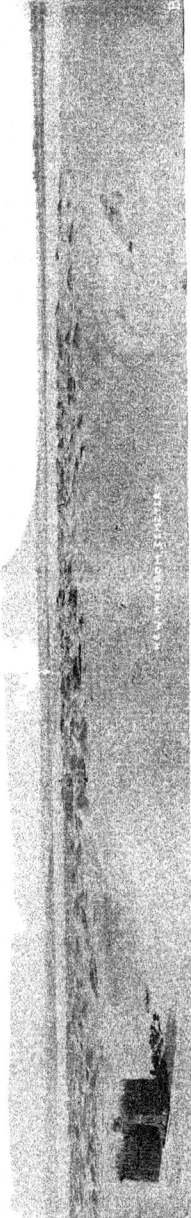

SOUTH.

EAST.

WEST.

EAST.

WEST.

H II

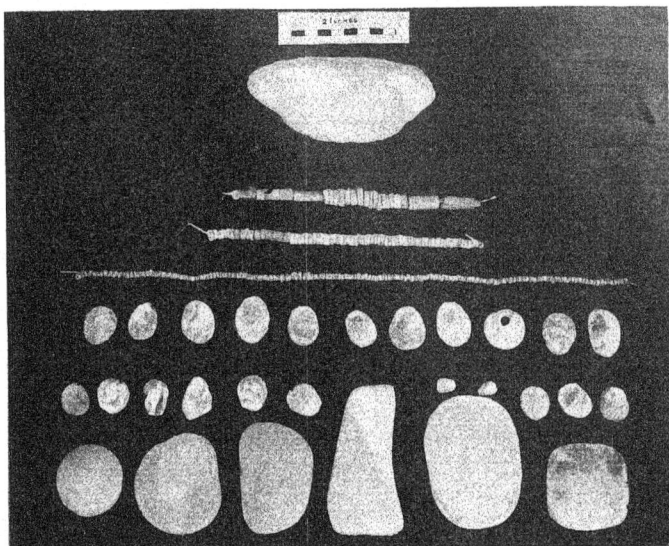

1. TOMB GROUP B 110.

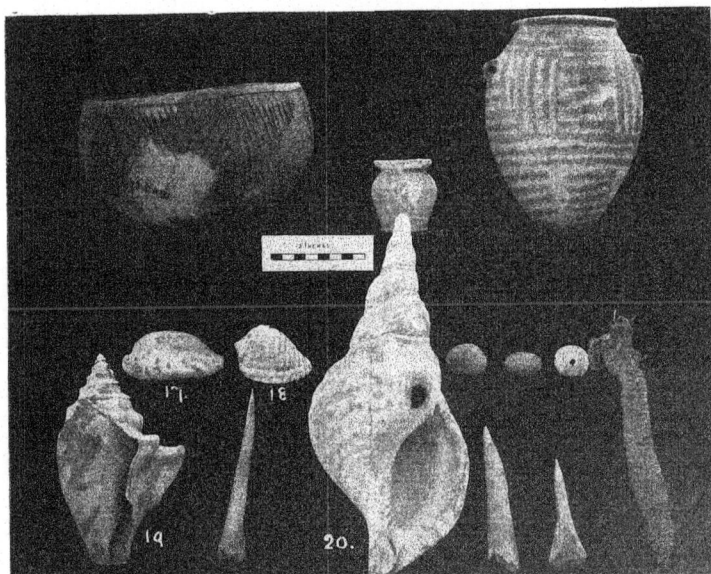

2. TOMB GROUP B 208.

TOMB GROUP B 185.

2. TOMB GROUP B 201.

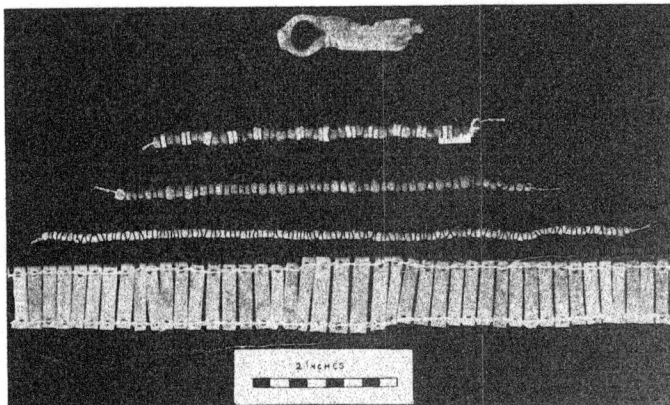

3. TOMB GROUP B 222.

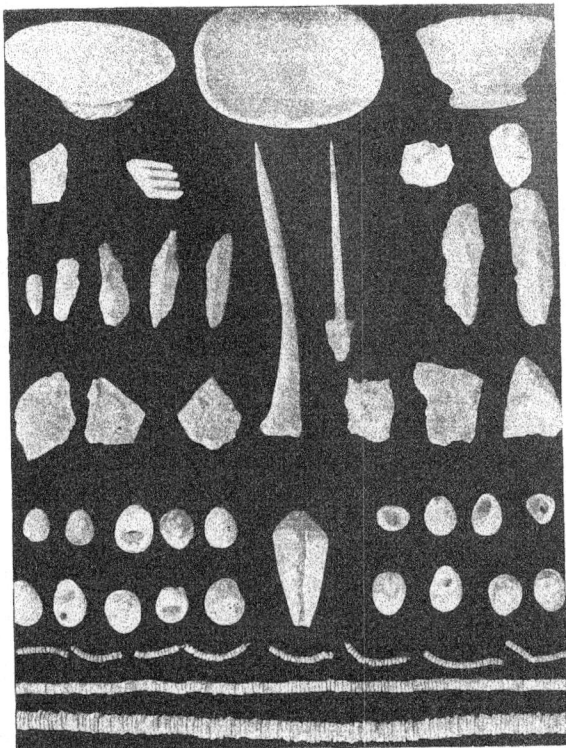

1. TOMB GROUP B 212.

2 INCHES

2. TOMB GROUP B 213.

1. BUFF, RED-POLISHED, AND HATCHED WARE.

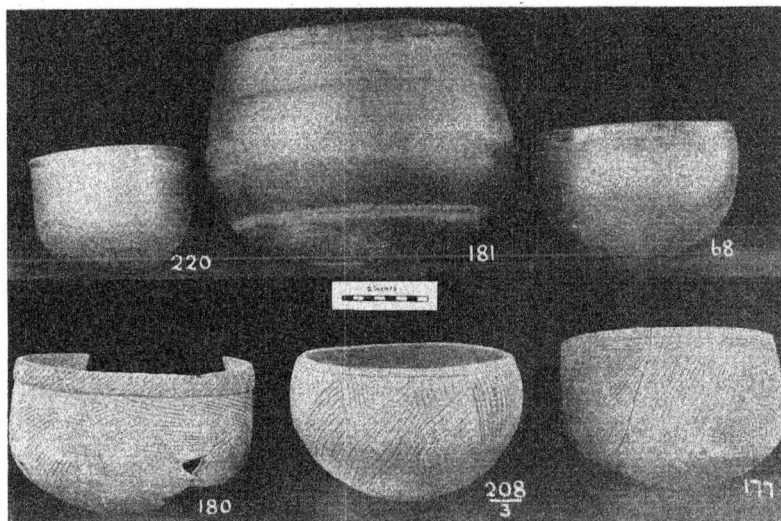

2. BLACK-TOPPED AND HATCHED WARE.

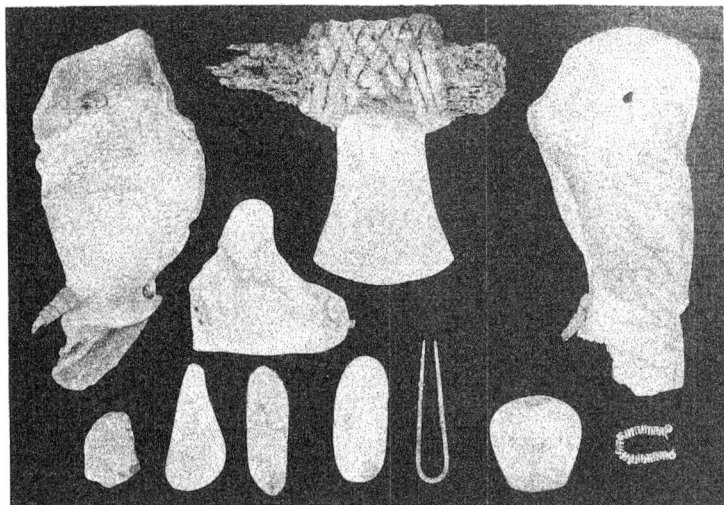

1. TOMB GROUP B 226.

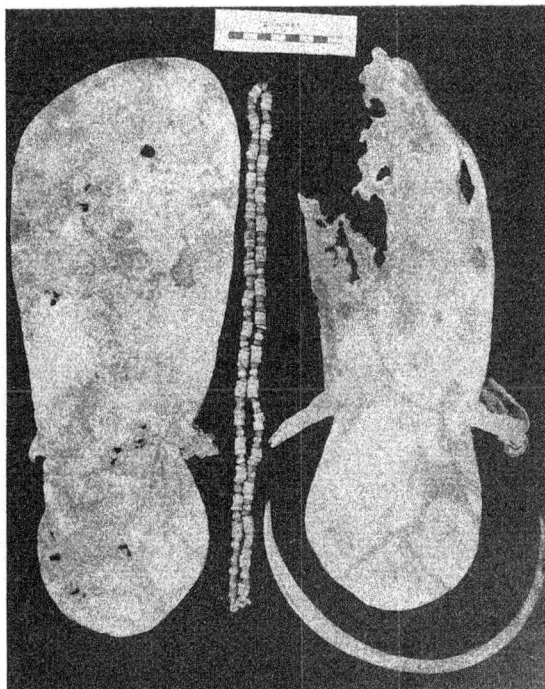

2. TOMB GROUP B 227.

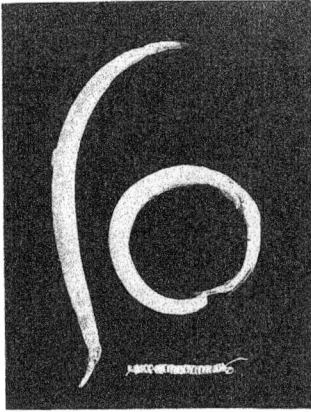

3. TOMB GROUP B 182.

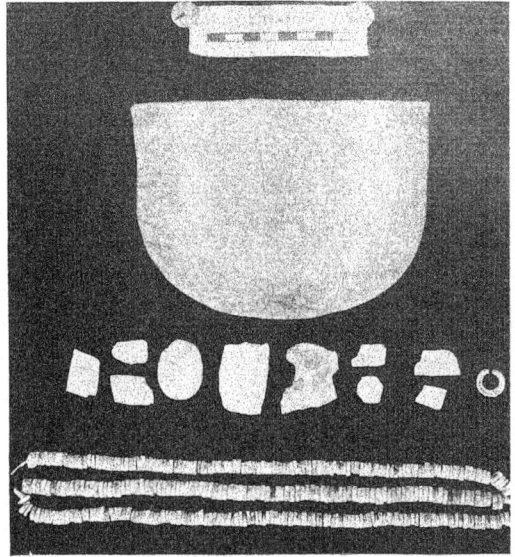

1. TOMB GROUP B 220.

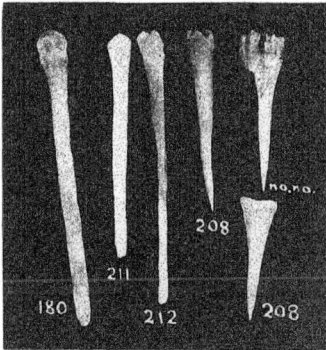

4. TYPES OF BONE BORERS AND SPATULAE.

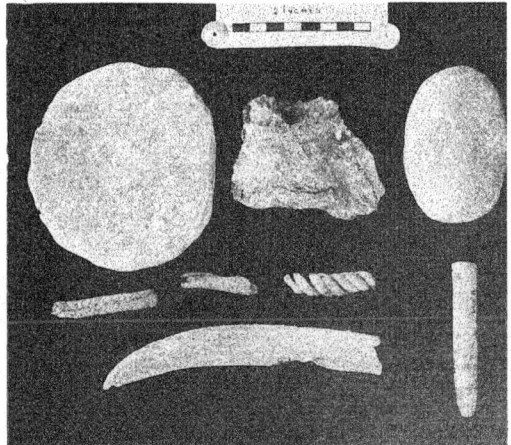

2. TOMB GROUP B 239.

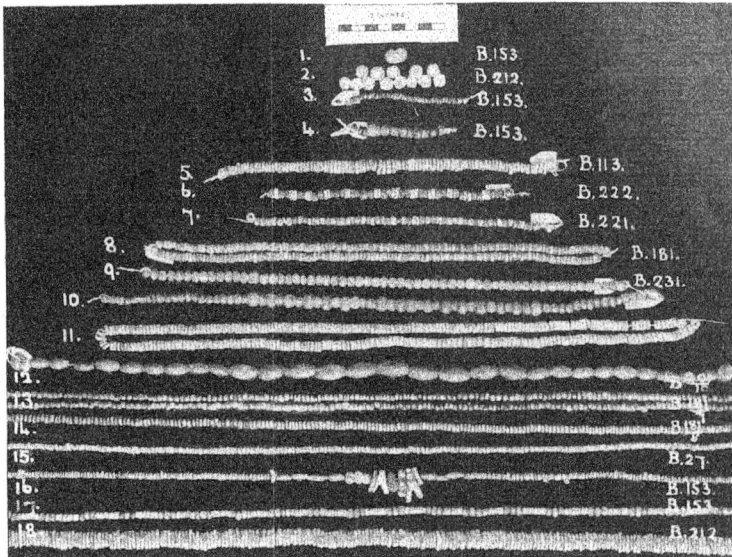

1. BEADS.

2. SHELLS.

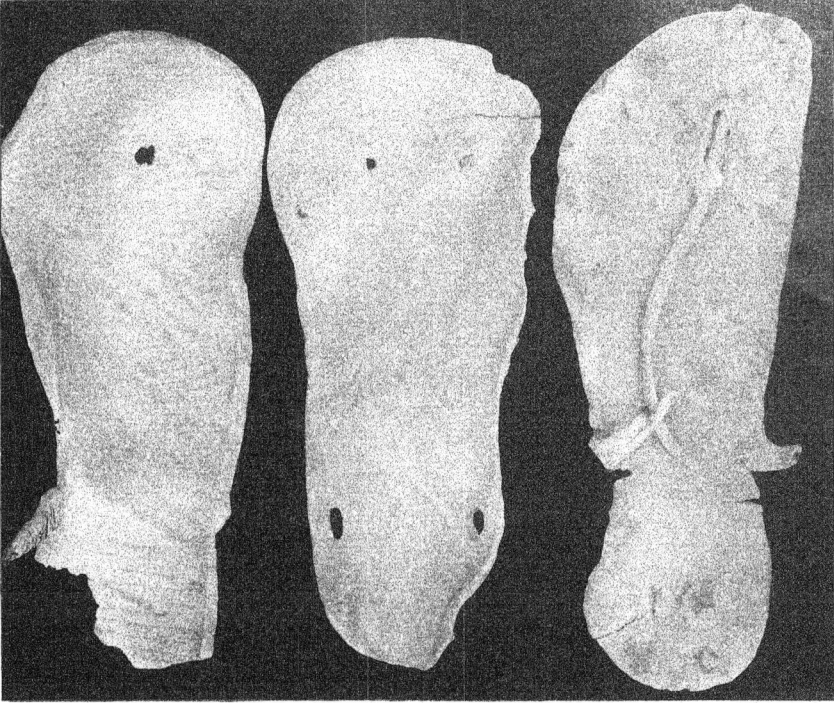

TYPE 1. B 226.   TYPE 2. B 218.   TYPE 3. B 234, 243.

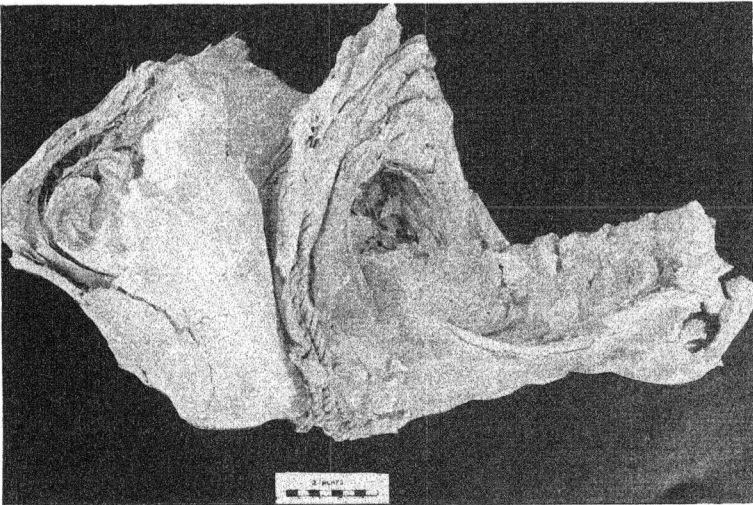

2. LEATHERN SKIRT. B 216.

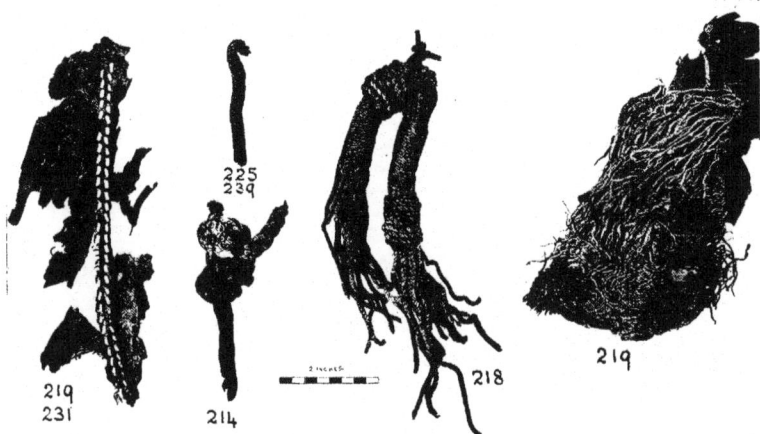

1. TYPES OF FRINGED LEATHER, BEADS SEWN INTO SEAMS, AND CORDAGE.

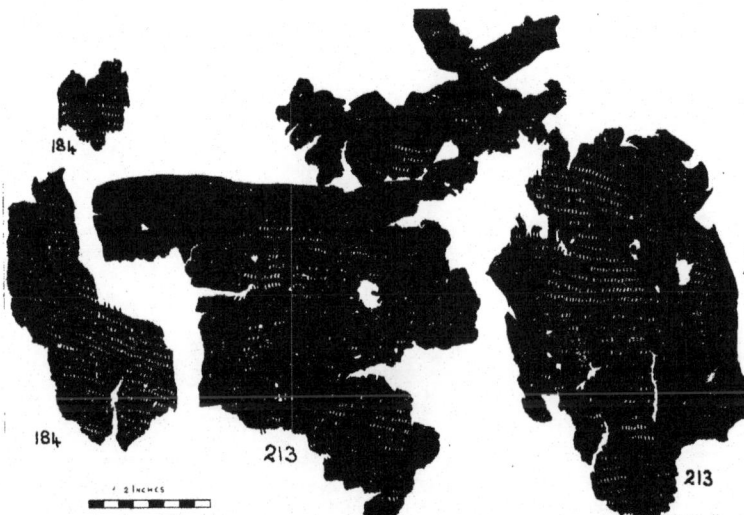

2 TYPES OF PIERCED LEATHER.

1. STITCHED LEATHER. B 179.

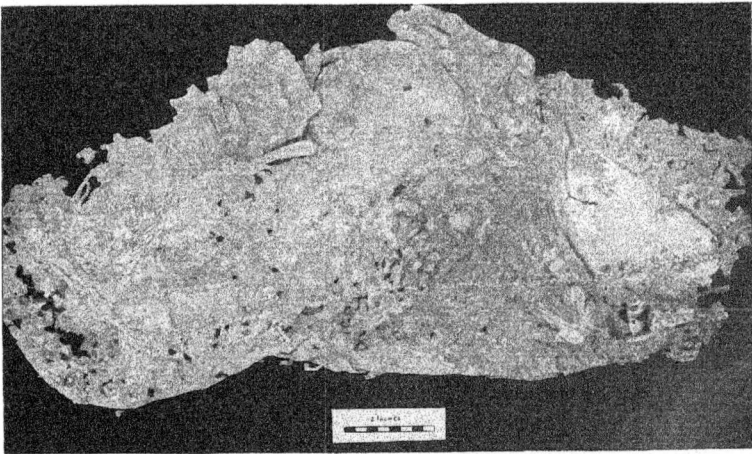

2. LEATHER BUNDLE WITH BEADS IN THE SEAMS. B 235.

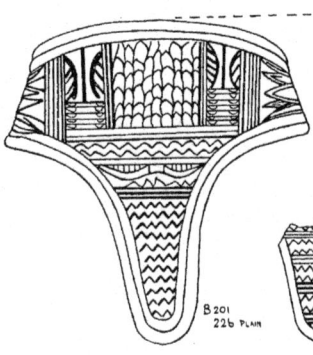

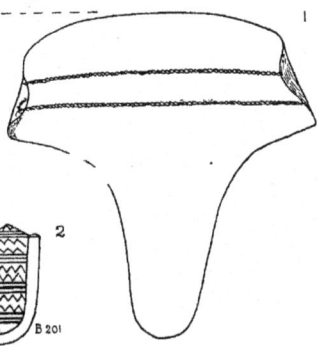

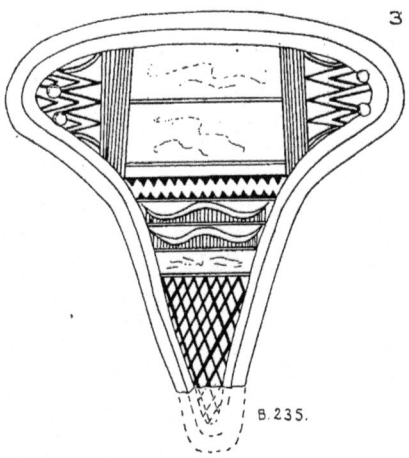

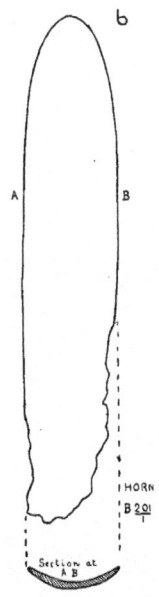

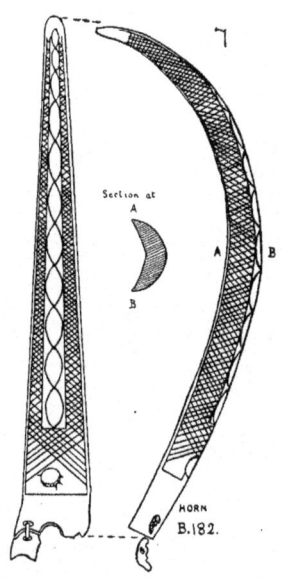

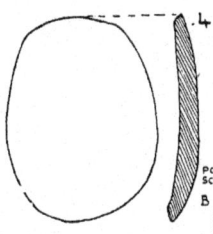

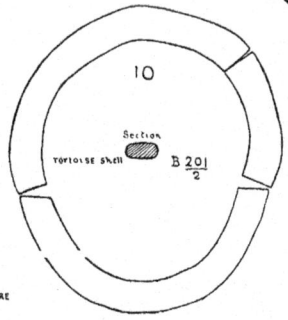

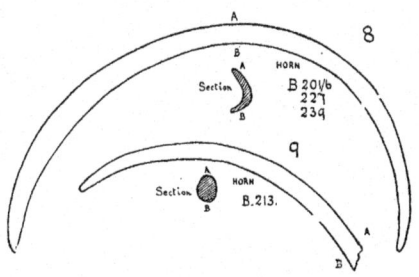

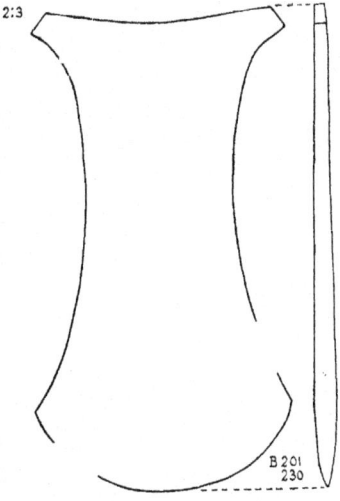

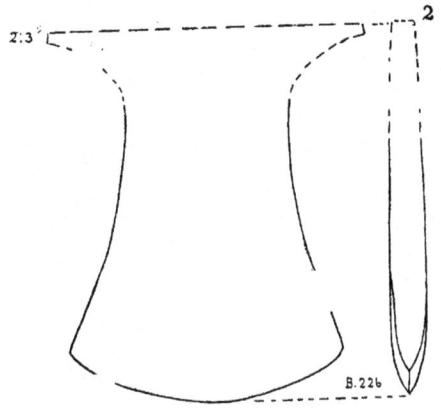

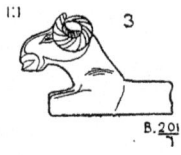

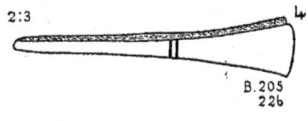

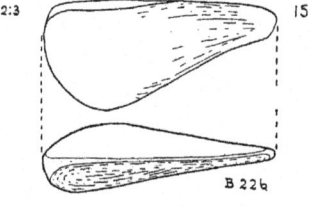

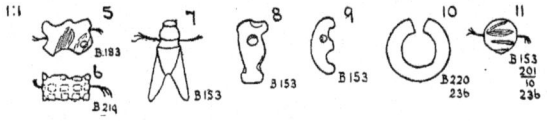

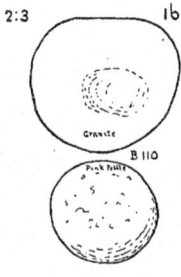

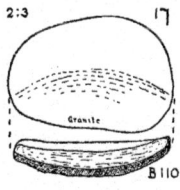

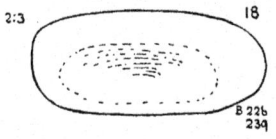

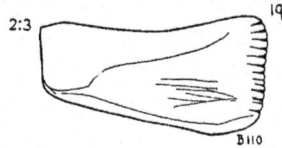

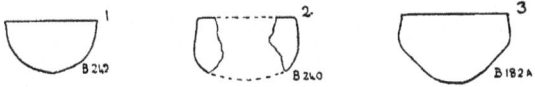

RED POLISHED WARE

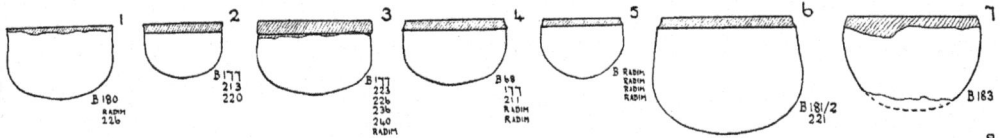

BLACK-TOPPED WARE B.

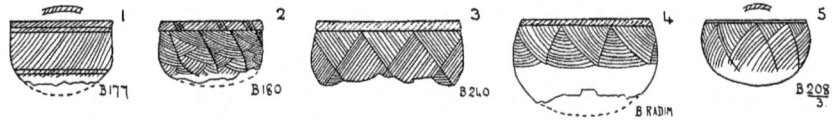

HATCHED WARE H

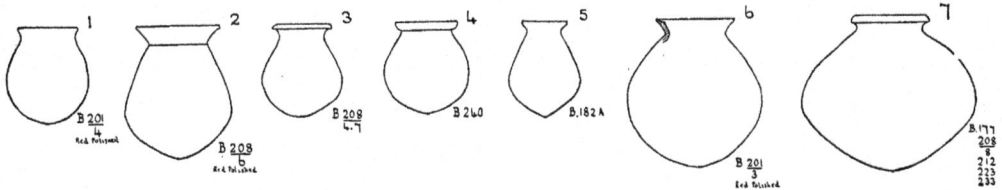

BUFF WARE.

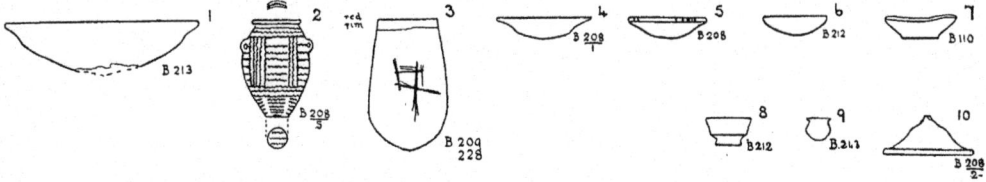

BORROWED POTTERY.

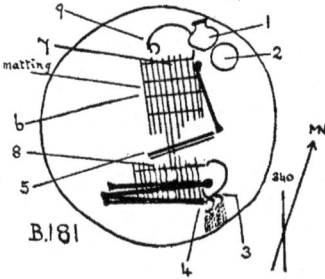

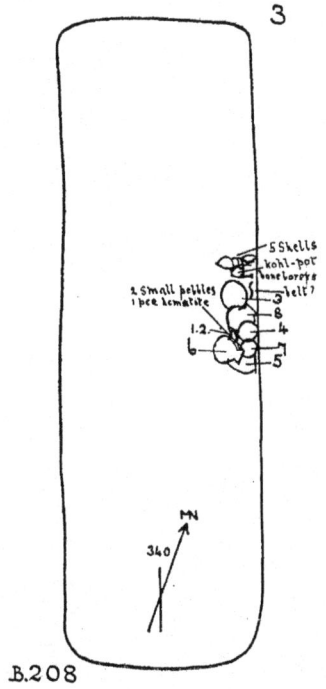

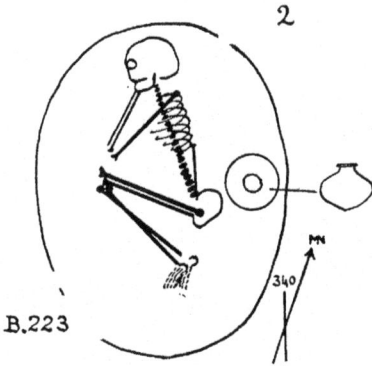

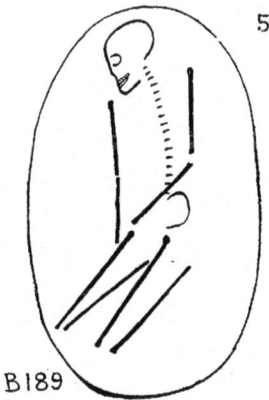

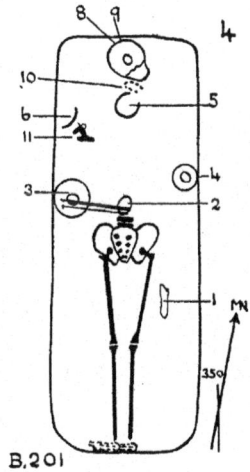

NOTE.—The Numbers are the Type Numbers, in the case of Beads on Plate VIII, Amulets Plate XII,
Shells Plate VIII, Pottery Plate XIV, Horn Plate XII, Kohl-pots Plate XIII, Sandals Plate IX.

CIRCULAR GRAVES.—CONTRACTED BURIALS.

NUMBER	GRAVE CONDITION	DIAMETER	DIAMETER	DEPTH	BODY HEAD	FACING	SEX	LEATHER COARSE	FINE	CLOTHING	CORDAGE	BEADS TYPE	TYPE	AMULETS SHELL STRIPS	SHELLS TYPE	POTTERY P	B	H	BUFF	BORROWED	HORN TYPE	KOHL POTS	BONE	COPPER	VARIOUS	REMARKS
110	P				NONE			×				1.18.2 3.17.18 14.			2.3.4 5.6.7 8.9.				7					PLATE	2 PALETTES. 1 RUBBER 8 NOTCHED PEBBLE 8 POTTERY SCRAPER	PALETTES WERE MERELY FLAT PEBBLES, NOTCHED PEBBLE IS A PALSTVE? LEATHER RETAINED ITS HAIR.
177	P	150	160	180			M	×	×		×				2.	2.3.4.	1	7							FINE LEATHER WAS DYED RED 8 LINED THE COARSE. BURIAL WAS BEEN WRAPPED IN THE LEATHER 8 TIED WITH THE CORD.
178	P	110	120	165	NONE							1.			SHERD										WOVEN MATERIAL COW 8 HORN	WEAVING PLAIN 8 LOOSE.
180	P	100	100	155	N	F		×							1.	1.	2				HUR-TH				A 3RD FEMUR SCENT OF OINTMENT SHEEPS LEG BONE	6 SHELLS OF THE ONE KIND. MUCH OF LEATHER DYED RED. MUCH SKIN 8 TISSUE ON BONES. LEATHER ALL W TROUT HAIR.
181	I	·95	·95	165	340°	W		WITH BLK WOOL				14.2. 3.12.24				6		8							WOVEN MATERIAL MAT PIERCED TYPE	GRAVE SLIGHTLY WIDER BELOW. BODY COVERED WITH THICK LAYER WOVEN MATERIAL, THEN WITH MAT. THICK PAD OF LEATHER UNDERNEATH.
182A	P	115	125	160	NONE			×		×		1				3		5							OINTMENT IN BUFF POT	LEATHER RETAINED 8 THE HAIR.
183	P	105	110	170			M	×	×		×	1.2.	5		15.16.		7			SCRAP BRACELET					WOVEN MATERIAL	HAIR ON FINE RED DYED LEATHER.
185	P	145	·125	170			M																		OX SKULL SPOTTED RED 8 BLACK. RAM'S HORN.	ANIMAL 8 HUMAN BONES JUMBLED TOGETHER.
202	P				NONE																	5.				BRACELETS WERE A PAIR.
212	P	140	140	120	NONE			×				13			1.2.3. 4.9.10 13?		7	6.8.			HAIR PIN BORER BORER SCRAPS				UNFINISHED BEADS OF TYPE 1. 7 FLINT FLAKES. LUMPS HEMATITE ? RED HEMATITE RUBBED. POTSHERD SCRAPER. MALACHITE.	HEMATITE LUMPS SHEWED A METALLIC LUSTRE. 8 LEATHER BONE INTO 8 WAS.
214	P	·95	·95	150	REMAINS of THREE				×						1.										MASS MIXED LEATHER WOVEN MATERIAL 8 FLINT	GRAVE CUT IN MARL. MUCH SKIN STILL ON SCATTERED BONES.
216	P						F	×		×	×															MUCH SKIN ON BONES. CORDAGE HERE ACCORDED USED.
218	P	100	100	170							×														PR SANDALS TYPE 2	46 BITS.
219	P	130	130	125	NONE				×	×		1.3.9	6.										14			CORD WOUND ROUND WAIST AS BELT. LEATHER AWLS 8 BEADS STITCHED INTO SEAMS, FRINGES.
220	P	110	110	120	30°	W	M					1.3			2.		'2.								CALCITE CRYSTALS. SHELL EARRING TYPE 10.	
222	P				NONE							1.3. 6.9.12.	STRIPS												SANDAL LOOP.	
224	I	120	110	110	20°	W	F?	×				1.														MUCH SKIN LEFT ON SKELETON CORD TIED OF BUNDLE OF LEATHER WITH BODY INSIDE.
225	P				NONE					×	×	1.													PCE. OF FLAT SAND STONE, PALETTE?	LEATHER WITH PIERCED PATTERN. CORD 8 PLAITED LEATHER. BRACELETS WERE A PAIR.
226	P	120	140	120	NONE			×	×			1.				1.3.							13?	AXE	PR SANDALS TYPE 1 2 UNSQUARED WIDE SMOOTH STONES. LOTUS IN CHAREAS.	AXE BOUND TO HANDLE BY HIDE THONGS. COARSE LEATHER UNDYED RETAINING HAIR. RED DYED LEATHER HAIRLESS.
230	P	140	140	160	NONE			×			×	25.			'SHERD		8.				STAIN ON PELVIS				WOVEN MATERIAL, 8 STUD CALCITE. MAT. TYPE 2 OVAL FLAT PEBBLE. ROLLER WARE SCRATCH 8 WOOD BOUND WITH LEATHER. AXE-HAFT?	WOVEN MATERIAL OF COARSE BROWN QUALITY. CORD OF PLAITED LEATHER, ALSO PLAIN TWIST. HAIR ON THE LEATHER. SKIN LEFT ON BONES. PEBBLE WAS A PALETTE?
240	P				NONE			×				1.AMULET POT. 1.2.				2	3	4							SCENT OF OINTMENT IN THE POT. BUFF 4.	HAIR ON THE LEATHER.

OVAL GRAVES.—CONTRACTED BURIALS.

NUMBER	GRAVE CONDITION	LENGTH	BREADTH	DEPTH	GRAVE AXIS	HEAD	FACING	SEX	COARSE	FINE	CLOTHING	CORDAGE	BEADS	SHELL STRIPS	SHELLS	P	B	H	BUFF	BORROWED	HORN	KOHL POTS	BONE	COPPER	VARIOUS	REMARKS
96	P	130	·80	140	NONE								21.22. 3	STRIPS	2·											
150	P	200	100	100	NONE								2. 3.													
176	P	120	·90	180	320° NONE								3.													GRAVE WHOLLY OF GRAVEL.
179	P	160	130	165	320°				×	×															YELLOW SKEW.	
184	I	140	110	100	300 SSW																					CHILD MILK TEETH NOT CUT. 2ND MOLAR ONLY LEFT.
204	P	130	·55	125	300° NONE										5											
210	I	140	·80	130	320°			F					2.												BEADS ON NECK.	
211	P	175	125	140	320° NONE				×						SHERD 4.8.						HAIR PIN				LUMP HEMATITE.	
213	P	150	120	110	310°			M	×	×	×		3.			2.									SEVERAL LARGE BLACK FEATHERS. ELEPHANT HAIR BAG. SHORT PLAITS of HAIR. 8 SMALL BLK PEBBLES. 1 - AGATE.	LEATHER WITH PIERCED PATTERN. NEAR PELVIS. FINE LEATHER DYED RED 8 LINED THE COARSE LEATHER. COARSE LEATHER RETAINED HAIR. STRIPS OF HIDE WITH HAIR ON.
223	I	130	100	105	340°	W			×			×				3									GREENSTONE HONE?	GRAVE CUT DOWN INTO MARL.
232	P	120	·70	110	340° NONE				×							3						13.				STRIP 170 WIDE AT S. END OF GRAVE. KOHL-POT OF BLUE MARBLE. HAIR ON THE LEATHER.
234	P	140	·70	125	335° NONE					×			3.												PR SANDALS TYPE 5.	BEADS STITCHED INTO LEATHER.
241	P	135	·60	130	320° NONE					×			1.2.12 23.1												SHORT PLAITS HAIR.	LATERAL NICHE 60 WIDE ON NE SIDE.

For explanation of reference numbers see Plate XVI.

LONG GRAVES.—EXTENDED BURIALS.

NUMBER	CONDITION	GRAVE LENGTH	BREADTH	DEPTH	HEAD AXIS	FACING	SEX	COARSE	FINE	CLOTHING	CORDAGE	BEADS TYPE	AMULETS SHELL STRIPS TYPE	SHELLS TYPE	P	B	H	BUFF	BORROWED	HORN TYPE	KOHL POTS TYPE	BONE	COPPER	VARIOUS	REMARKS
27	P	270	100	200								3.													
68	P	300	100	160											4										
98	P	270	100	160								1.2													
153	P	250	125	205								3.5 10. 7 8.9 11.12.14. 21.												TYPE 3 BEADS OF BLUE DARK GREENISH COLOUR.
184	P	210	100	170						×															LEATHER WITH PIECES OF COTTON ON THIGHS. SKIN ALMOST INTACT.
188	P	210	105	160																					LATERAL NICHE ON SIDE. MUCH SKIN LEFT.
195	P	210	65	145	330°							3.													
201	P	165	60	170	350°		M	×	×			3. 21.				4.	6.		5.6.8.	14.			AXE RAM	PORTAISE SKULL BEATD DRY. WAISTGUARD. YELLOW SINEW BANDLES. WOVEN MATERIAL. STRING SIGHT OF OINTMENT IN BOTH POTS.	KOHL POT SUPPLIED WITH POTTERY COVER. CARNELIAN BEADS AT NECK. FINE LEATHER DYED RED. TYPE 3 BEADS SEWN ON. BURIAL LYING ON FACE & COVERED WITH LEATHER UNDER MATERIAL. MILKED LEGS. WEE BACK UPWARDS
205	P											1.												DRESSER	
207	P	225	100	130								2.								12.				KOHL. POT SUPPLIED WITH COVER RUBBED DOWN FROM POTSHERD. SHELLS STRUNG ON LEATHER.
208	P	225	80	190	340°				×			15? 17.18. 19.20.			5.	3.2. 3.7.	2.4. 5.10.		13?	3 BORERS			WOVEN BELT? 1 SCRAP OF HEMATITE 2 SMALL PEBBLES SCENT OF OINTMENT SCRAPER OF POTTERY	KOHL POT OF BLUE MARBLE BROKEN. BORDERED POT 2 IS PRE-DYNASTIC. LEATHER IN COVER OF POT BUFF? AS BINDING?
230	P	280	110	160	340°			×				1.											AXE	2 SHEE P LEG BONES	MUCH SKIN LEFT ON BONES. LEATHER WITH HAIR ON IT.
231	I	210	90	135	320°		F		×			1.3.0.			2.									LEATHER WITH FRINGE	TYPE 0 BEADS AT NECK. OTHERS SEWN IN LEATHER.
235	P	180	90	160	315°		M	×		×		1.3.			2.									WOVEN MATERIAL. MAT PIERCED TYPE SCRAPS SOME THING HARD SEWN DOWN LEATHER. WAISTGUARD.	BLUE & WHITE BEADS TYPES 1.3. SEWN INTO LEATHER. THIS BUNDLE OF LEATHER COVERED BY LINEN & AGAIN BY MAT. PARTS OF 3 SKELETONS. CORD PLAIN TWIST. VERY FINE CORDS TO WAISTGUARD.
238	I	180	80	80	320°		F			×														MAT. TYPE 2. COARSE QUALITY WOVEN MATERIAL.	LAID ON FACE. WRAPPED IN CLOTH. MAT LAID ON, & CH "HENNA" PASTE COATED THE WHOLE. SKIN WELL PRESERVED, DYED RED. HAIR IN SHORT THIN PLAITS. NO MAT OF "HENNA" BENEATH BODY. 3 LEATHER CORDS AS AT LEFT.

DEPOSITS WITHOUT BURIALS.

NUMBER	CONDITION							COARSE	FINE			BEADS			P	B	H	BUFF	BORROWED					VARIOUS	REMARKS
182	SMALL TRIANGULAR HOLE								1.						9			5.7.						OINTMENT IN POT.	HOLE ONLY JUST DEEP ENOUGH TO CONTAIN POT. FEW BEADS HAD ONCE BEEN SEWN INTO LEATHER, POT WRAPPED IN CLOTH.
233	SMALL IRREGULAR HOLE																							OINTMENT IN POT.	POT WAS SEALED & CRACKED WITH OINTMENT.

SUNDRY "PAN-GRAVE" GROUPS.

NUMBER	CONDITION							COARSE	FINE			BEADS	AMULETS	SHELLS	P	B	H	BUFF	BORROWED					VARIOUS	REMARKS
221	P											1.3.10.			6.										1 PR SANDALS.TYPE 1.	LEATHER BUNDLE WITHOUT HAIR.
227	P											1.12.13.						8.							
228	P											1.3.13.						3							
236	P		SKULL ONLY LEFT				×					1.3.15.	2.6.	3.										1 SHELL EARRING TYPE 10.	PCE SLATE CHIPPED ROUND EDGES. BLUE BEADS SEWN ONTO LEATHER.
262	P											1.2.3. 6.12.													SANDAL TYPE 3? PALETTE OF BROKEN PCE YELLOW SANDSTONE. 104 RIB.	MUCH SKIN ON REMAINING BONES. GREEN PAINT STAINS ON PALETTE. LEATHER DYED RED.
263	P																	9.							

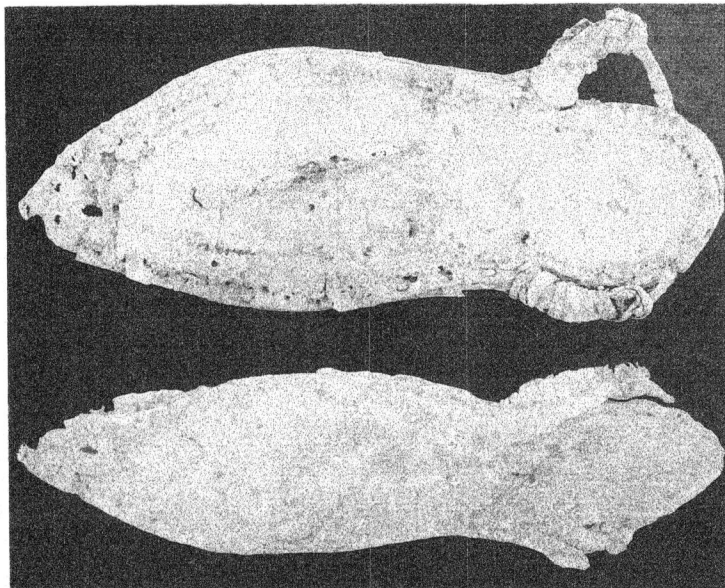

1. TWO VIEWS OF A SANDAL. B 170.

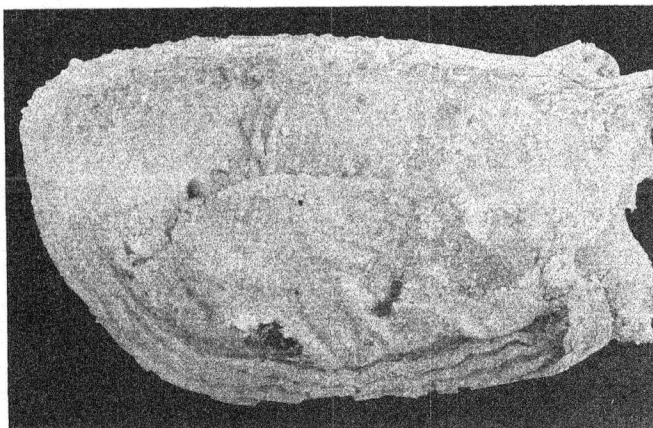

2. FOREPART OF A SHOE-SANDAL. B 15.

1. POT WITH PIERCED PROTUBERANCES.

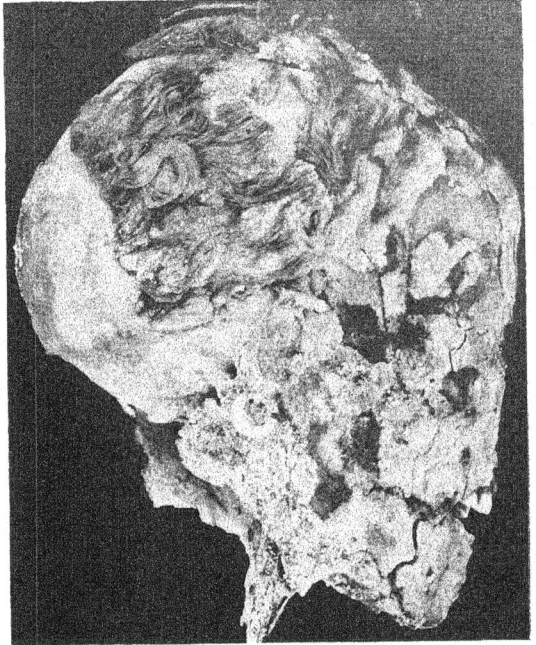

2. PENANNULAR EARRING IN POSITION. B 66.

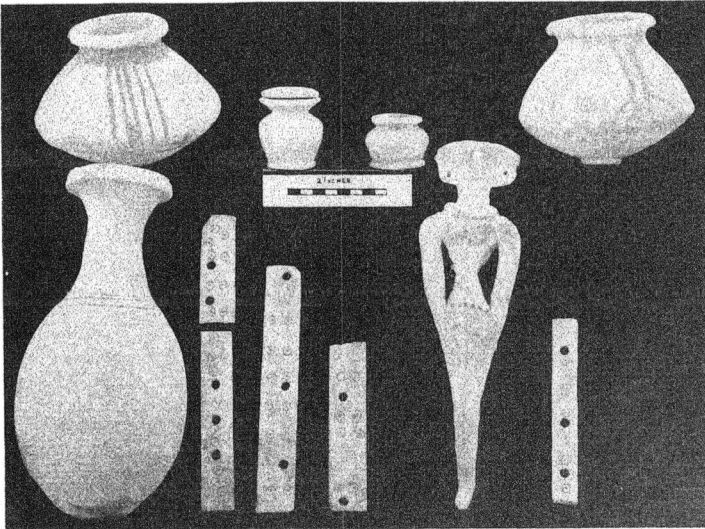

3. TOMB GROUP B 154.

PLATE XX.

BALABISH.   GROUP B101 AND THREE VIEWS OF THE FIGURE VASE.   LATE XVIIIth DYNASTY.

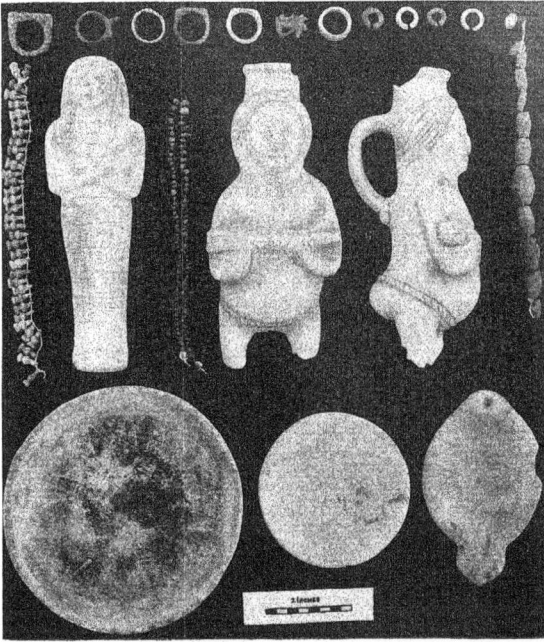

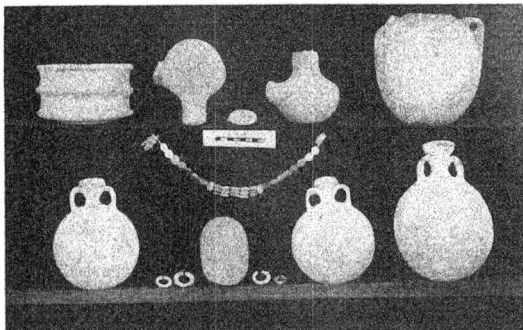

1. TOMB GROUP B 50. TWO POTS WITH HUMAN HEADS.

2. TOMB GROUP B 36.   FIGURE VASE. CANOPIC JAR COVERS? USHABTIS?

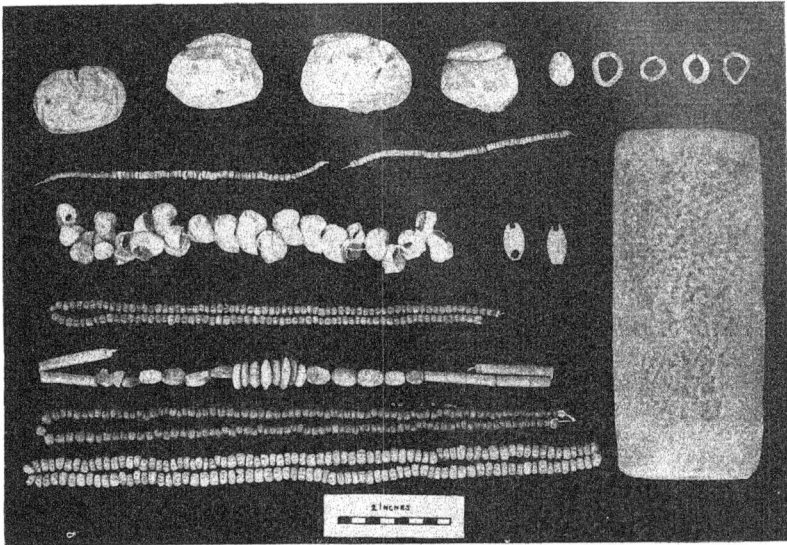

1. TOMB GROUP B 90.

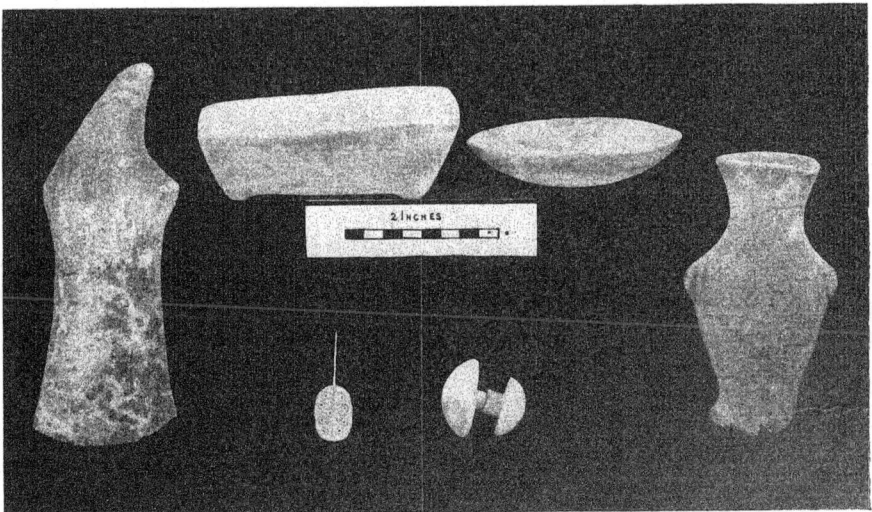

2. TOMB GROUP B 157.

SCALE OF VASES 1:6
,,   ,, SCARAB 1:1

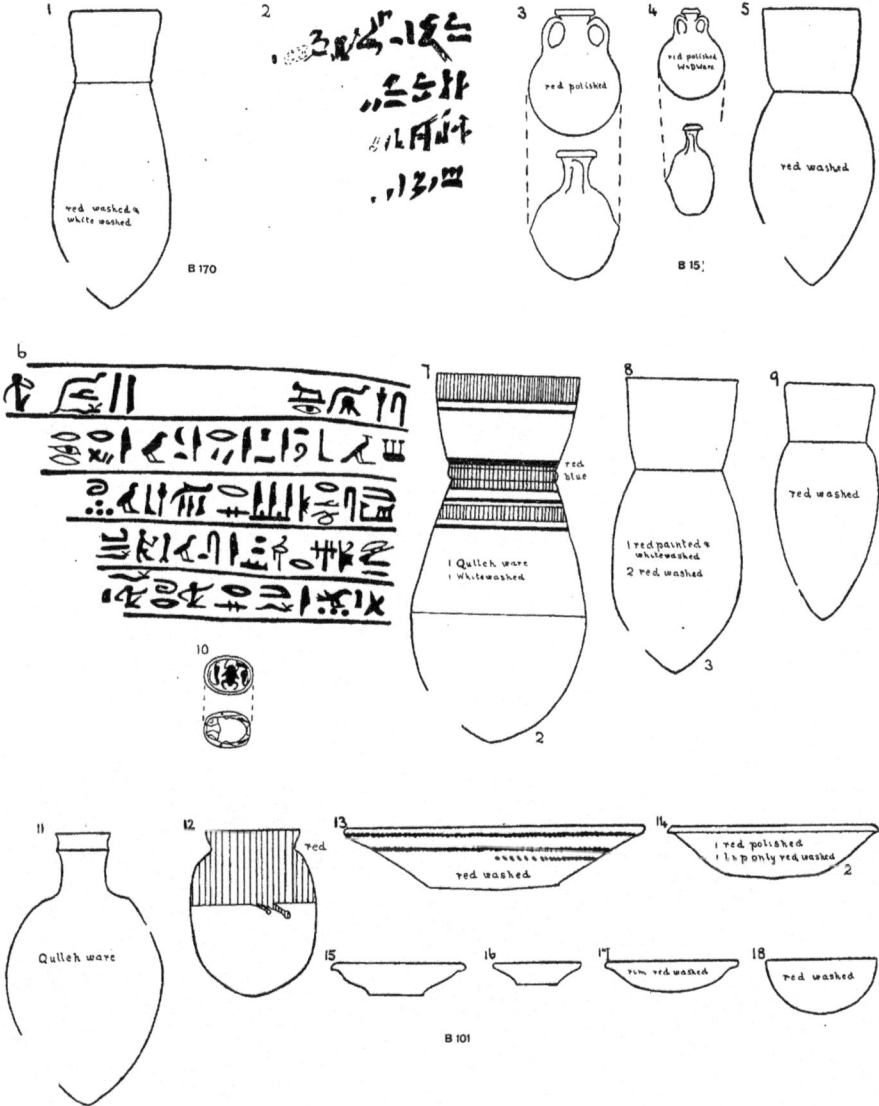

The figure at the foot of a pot indicates the number of that type found in the grave.

SCALE OF VASES 1:6
„   „ SCARABS 1:1

The figure at the foot of a pot indicates the number of that type found in the grave.

SCALE: POTTERY 1:6
OTHER OBJECTS 2:3

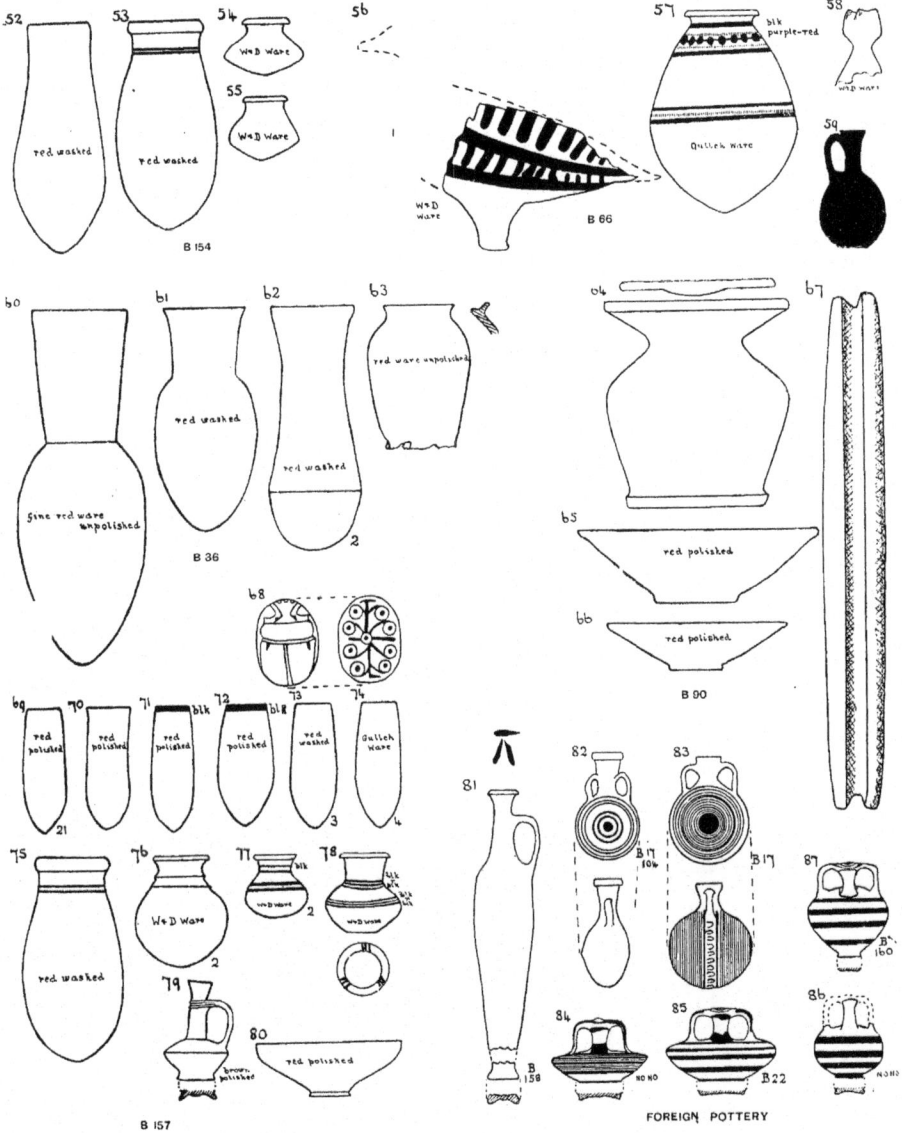

The figure at the foot of a pot indicates the number of that type found in the grave.

PUBLICATIONS OF THE EGYPT EXPLORATION SOCIETY.

EXCAVATION MEMOIRS.

I.—THE STORE CITY OF PITHOM AND THE ROUTE OF THE EXODUS. By EDOUARD NAVILLE. 13 Plates and Plans. (Fourth and Revised Edition, 1888.) 25s.

II.—TANIS. Part I. By W. M. FLINDERS PETRIE. 18 Plates and 2 Plans. (Second Edition, 1889.) 25s.

III.—NAUKRATIS. Part I. By W. M. FLINDERS PETRIE. With Chapters by CECIL SMITH, ERNEST A. GARDNER, and BARCLAY V. HEAD. 44 Plates and Plans. (Second Edition, 1888.) 25s.

IV.—GOSHEN, AND THE SHRINE OF SAFT-EL-HENNEH. By EDOUARD NAVILLE. 11 Plates and Plans. (Second Edition, 1886.) 25s.

V.—TANIS. Part II, including TELL DEFENNEH (the Biblical "Tahpanhes") and TELL NEBESHEH. By W. M. FLINDERS PETRIE, F. LL. GRIFFITH, and A. S. MURRAY. 51 Plates and Plans. 1888. (Out of print.)

VI.—NAUKRATIS. Part II. By ERNEST A. GARDNER and F. LL. GRIFFITH. 24 Plates and Plans. 1888. (Out of print.)

VII.—THE CITY OF ONIAS AND THE MOUND OF THE JEW. The Antiquities of Tell-el-Yahûdiyeh. By EDOUARD NAVILLE and F. LL. GRIFFITH. 26 Plates and Plans. 1890. 25s.

VIII.—BUBASTIS. By EDOUARD NAVILLE. 54 Plates. (Second Edition, 1891.) 25s.

IX.—TWO HIEROGLYPHIC PAPYRI FROM TANIS. Containing:
THE SIGN PAPYRUS (a Syllabary). By F. LL. GRIFFITH.
THE GEOGRAPHICAL PAPYRUS (an Almanac). By W. M. FLINDERS PETRIE. With Remarks by HEINRICH BRUGSCH. 1889. (Out of print.)

X.—THE FESTIVAL HALL OF OSORKON II (BUBASTIS). By EDOUARD NAVILLE. 39 Plates. 1892. 25s.

XI.—AHNAS EL MEDINEH. By EDOUARD NAVILLE. 18 Plates; and THE TOMB OF PAHERI AT EL KAB. By J. J. TYLOR and F. LL. GRIFFITH. 10 Plates. 1894. 25s.

XII.—DEIR EL BAHARI. Introductory. By EDOUARD NAVILLE. 15 Plates and Plans. 1894. 25s.

XIII.—DEIR EL BAHARI. Part I. By EDOUARD NAVILLE. Plates I-XXIV (3 coloured), with Description. Royal folio. 1895. 30s.

XIV.—DEIR EL BAHARI. Part II. By EDOUARD NAVILLE. Plates XXV-LV (2 coloured), with Description. Royal folio. 1897. 30s.

XV.—DESHÂSHEH. By W. M. FLINDERS PETRIE. Photogravure and other Plates. 1898. 25s.

XVI.—DEIR EL BAHARI. Part III. By EDOUARD NAVILLE. Plates LVI-LXXXVI (2 coloured), with Description. Royal folio. 1898. 30s.

XVII.—DENDEREH. By W. M. FLINDERS PETRIE. 38 Plates. 1900. 25s. (Extra Plates of Inscriptions. 40 Plates. 10s.)

XVIII.—ROYAL TOMBS OF THE FIRST DYNASTY. By W. M. FLINDERS PETRIE. 68 Plates. 1900. 25s.

XIX.—DEIR EL BAHARI. Part IV. By EDOUARD NAVILLE. Plates LXXXVII-CXVIII (2 coloured), with Description. Royal folio. 1901. 30s.

XX.—DIOSPOLIS PARVA. By W. M. FLINDERS PETRIE. 49 Plates. 1901. (Out of print.)

XXI.—THE ROYAL TOMBS OF THE EARLIEST DYNASTIES. Part II. By W. M. FLINDERS PETRIE. 63 Plates. 1901. 25s. (35 extra Plates. 10s.)

XXII.—ABYDOS. Part I. By W. M. FLINDERS PETRIE. 81 Plates. 1902. 25s.

XXIII.—EL AMRAH AND ABYDOS. By D. RANDALL-MacIVER, A. C. MACE, and F. LL. GRIFFITH. 60 Plates. 1902. 25s.

XXIV.—ABYDOS. Part II. By W. M. FLINDERS PETRIE. 64 Plates. 1903. 25s.

XXV.—ABYDOS. Part III. By C. T. CURRELLY, E. R. AYRTON, and A. E. P. WEIGALL, &c. 61 Plates. 1904. 25s.

XXVI.—EHNASYA. By W. M. FLINDERS PETRIE. 43 Plates. 1905. 25s. (ROMAN EHNASYA. 32 extra Plates. 10s.)

XXVII.—DEIR EL BAHARI. Part V. By EDOUARD NAVILLE. Plates CXIX-CL, with Description. Royal folio. 1906. 30s.

XXVIII.—THE XIth DYNASTY TEMPLE AT DEIR EL BAHARI. Part I. By EDOUARD NAVILLE, H. R. HALL, and E. R. AYRTON. 31 Plates. 1907. (Out of print.)

XXIX.—DEIR EL BAHARI. Part VI. By EDOUARD NAVILLE. Plates CLI-CLXXIV (1 coloured), with Description. Royal folio. 1908. 30s.

XXX.—THE XIth DYNASTY TEMPLE AT DEIR EL BAHARI. Part II. By EDOUARD NAVILLE and SOMERS CLARKE. 24 Plates. 1910. 25s.

XXXI.—PRE-DYNASTIC CEMETERY AT EL MAHASNA. By E. R. AYRTON and W. L. S. LOAT. 1911. 25s.

XXXII.—THE XIth DYNASTY TEMPLE AT DEIR EL BAHARI. Part III. By EDOUARD NAVILLE, H. R. HALL, and C. T. CURRELLY. 36 Plates. 1913. 25s.

XXXIII.—CEMETERIES OF ABYDOS. Part I. By EDOUARD NAVILLE, T. E. PEET, H. R. HALL, and K. HADDON. 1914. 25s.

XXXIV.—CEMETERIES OF ABYDOS. Part II. By T. E. PEET. 1914. 25s.

XXXV.—CEMETERIES OF ABYDOS. Part III. By T. E. PEET and W. L. S. LOAT. 1913. 25s.

XXXVI.—INSCRIPTIONS OF SINAI. Part I. By A. H. GARDINER and T. E. PEET. 86 Plates and Plans. Royal folio. 1917. 35s.

XXXVII.—BALABISH. By G. A. WAINWRIGHT. Preface by T. WHITTEMORE. 25 Plates. 1920. 42s.

SPECIAL PUBLICATIONS.

ΛΟΓΙΑ ΙΗΣΟΥ: "Sayings of Our Lord," from an Early Greek Papyrus. By B. P. GRENFELL and A. S. HUNT. 1897. (Out of print.)

NEW SAYINGS OF JESUS AND FRAGMENT OF A LOST GOSPEL, with the text of the "Logia" discovered in 1897. By B. P. GRENFELL and A. S. HUNT. 1904. 1s. net.

FRAGMENT OF AN UNCANONICAL GOSPEL. By B. P. GRENFELL and A. S. HUNT. 1908. 1s. net.

COPTIC OSTRACA. By W. E. CRUM. 1902. 10s. 6d. net.

THE THEBAN TOMBS SERIES. Vol. I. THE TOMB OF AMENEMHÊT (No. 82). By NINA DE G. DAVIES and A. H. GARDINER. 1915. 30s.

THE THEBAN TOMBS SERIES. Vol. II. THE TOMB OF ANTEFOKER. By NORMAN DE GARIS DAVIES and ALAN H. GARDINER. 1920. 42s.

THE MAYER PAPYRI A & B. By T. E. PEET. 1920. 42s.

OFFICES OF THE EGYPT EXPLORATION SOCIETY: 13, Tavistock Square, London, W.C. and 503, Tremont Temple, Boston, Mass., U.S.A.

PUBLICATIONS OF THE EGYPT EXPLORATION SOCIETY

ARCHAEOLOGICAL SURVEY.
Edited by F. LL. GRIFFITH.

I.—BENI HASAN. Part I. By PERCY E.
NEWBERRY. With Plans by G. W. FRASER. 49 Plates
(4 coloured). 1893. (Out of print.)

II.—BENI HASAN. Part II. By PERCY E.
NEWBERRY. With Appendix, Plans, and Measure-
ments by G. W. FRASER. 37 Plates (2 coloured).
1894. 25s.

III.—EL BERSHEH. Part I. By PERCY E.
NEWBERRY. 34 Plates (2 coloured). 1894. 25s.

IV.—EL BERSHEH. Part II. By F. LL. GRIFFITH
and PERCY E. NEWBERRY. With Appendix by G. W.
FRASER. 23 Plates (2 coloured). 1895. 25s.

V.—BENI HASAN. Part III. By F. LL. GRIFFITH.
(Hieroglyphs and Manufacture, &c., of Flint Knives.)
10 Coloured Plates. 1896. 25s.

VI.—HIEROGLYPHS FROM THE COLLECTIONS
OF THE EGYPT EXPLORATION FUND. By
F. LL. GRIFFITH. 9 Coloured Plates. 1898. 25s

VII.—BENI HASAN. Part IV. By F. LL. GRIFFITH.
(Illustrating Beasts and Birds, Arts, Crafts, &c.)
27 Plates (21 coloured). 1900. 25s.

VIII.—THE MASTABA OF PTAHHETEP AND
AKHETHETEP AT SAQQAREH. Part I. By
NORMAN DE G. DAVIES and F. LL. GRIFFITH. 31
Plates (3 coloured). 1900. 25s.

IX.—THE MASTABA OF PTAHHETEP AND
AKHETHETEP AT SAQQAREH. Part II. By
N. DE G. DAVIES and F. LL. GRIFFITH. 35 Plates.
1901. 25s.

X.—THE ROCK TOMBS OF SHEIKH SAID.
By N. DE G. DAVIES. 35 Plates. 1901. 25s.

XI.—THE ROCK TOMBS OF DEIR EL GEB-
RÂWI. Part I. By N. DE G. DAVIES. 27 Plates.
(2 coloured). 1902. 25s.

XII.—DEIR EL GEBRÂWI. Part II. By N. DE G.
DAVIES. 30 Plates (2 coloured). 1902. 25s.

XIII.—THE ROCK TOMBS OF EL AMARNA. Part I.
By N. DE G. DAVIES. 41 Plates. 1903. 25s.

XIV.—EL AMARNA. Part II. By N. DE G.
DAVIES. 47 Plates. 1905. 25s.

XV.—EL AMARNA. Part III. By N. DE G.
DAVIES. 40 Plates. 1905. 25s.

XVI.—EL AMARNA. Part IV. By N. DE G.
DAVIES. 45 Plates. 1906. 25s.

XVII.—EL AMARNA. Part V. By N. DE G.
DAVIES. 44 Plates. 1908. 25s.

XVIII.—EL AMARNA. Part VI. By N. DE G.
DAVIES. 44 Plates. 1908. 25s.

XIX.—THE ISLAND OF MEROË, by J. W. CROW-
FOOT, and MEROITIC INSCRIPTIONS, Part I, by
F. LL. GRIFFITH. 35 Plates. 1911. 25s.

XX.—MEROITIC INSCRIPTIONS. Part II. By
F. LL. GRIFFITH. 48 Plates. 1912. 25s.

XXI.—FIVE THEBAN TOMBS. By N. DE G.
DAVIES. 43 Plates. 1913. 25s.

XXII.—THE ROCK TOMBS OF MEIR. Part I.
By A. M. BLACKMAN. 33 Plates. 1914. 25s.

XXIII.—THE ROCK TOMBS OF MEIR. Part II.
By A. M. BLACKMAN. 35 Plates. 1915. 25s.

XXIV.—THE ROCK TOMBS OF MEIR. Part III.
By A. M. BLACKMAN. 39 Plates. 1915. 25s.

GRAECO-ROMAN MEMOIRS.

I.—THE OXYRHYNCHUS PAPYRI. Part I. By
B. P. GRENFELL and A. S. HUNT. 8 Collotype Plates.
1898. (Out of print.)

II.—THE OXYRHYNCHUS PAPYRI. Part II. By
B. P. GRENFELL and A. S. HUNT. 8 Collotype Plates.
1899. 25s.

III.—FAYÛM TOWNS AND THEIR PAPYRI. By
B. P. GRENFELL, A. S. HUNT, and D. G. HOGARTH.
18 Plates. 1900. 25s.

IV.—THE TEBTUNIS PAPYRI. By. B. P.
GRENFELL, A. S. HUNT, and J. G. SMYLY. 9 Collotype
Plates. 1902. (Not for Sale.)

V.—THE OXYRHYNCHUS PAPYRI. Part III.
By B. P. GRENFELL and A. S. HUNT. 6 Collotype
Plates. 1903. 25s.

VI.—THE OXYRHYNCHUS PAPYRI. Part IV.
By B. P. GRENFELL and A. S. HUNT. 8 Collotype
Plates. 1904. 25s.

VII.—THE HIBEH PAPYRI. Part I. By B. P.
GRENFELL and A. S. HUNT. 10 Collotype Plates.
1906. 45s.

VIII.—THE OXYRHYNCHUS PAPYRI. Part V.
By B. P. GRENFELL and A. S. HUNT. 7 Collotype
Plates. 1908. 25s.

IX.—THE OXYRHYNCHUS PAPYRI. Part VI.
By B. P. GRENFELL and A. S. HUNT. 6 Collotype
Plates. 1908. 25s.

X.—THE OXYRHYNCHUS PAPYRI. Part VII.
By A. S. HUNT. 6 Collotype Plates. 1910. 25s.

XI.—THE OXYRHYNCHUS PAPYRI. Part VIII.
By A. S. HUNT. 7 Collotype Plates. 1911. 25s.

XII.—THE OXYRHYNCHUS PAPYRI. Part IX.
By A. S. HUNT. 6 Collotype Plates. 1912. 25s.

XIII.—THE OXYRHYNCHUS PAPYRI. Part X.
By B. P. GRENFELL and A. S. HUNT. 6 Collotype
Plates. 1914. 25s.

XIV.—THE OXYRHYNCHUS PAPYRI. Part XI.
By B. P. GRENFELL and A. S. HUNT. 7 Collotype
Plates. 1915. 25s.

XV.—THE OXYRHYNCHUS PAPYRI. Part XII.
By B. P. GRENFELL and A. S. HUNT. 2 Collotype
Plates. 1916. 25s.

XVI.—THE OXYRHYNCHUS PAPYRI. Part XIII.
By B. P. GRENFELL and A. S. HUNT. 6 Collotype
Plates. 1919. 25s.

XVII.—THE OXYRHYNCHUS PAPYRI. Part XIV.
By B. P. GRENFELL and A. S. HUNT. 3 Collotype
Plates. 1920. 42s.

XVIII.—THE OXYRHYNCHUS PAPYRI. Part XV.
By B. P. GRENFELL, and A. S. HUNT. (In prepara-
tion.)

ANNUAL ARCHAEOLOGICAL REPORTS.

(Yearly Summaries by F. G. KENYON, W. E. CRUM, and the Officers of the Society, with Maps.)
Edited by F. LL. GRIFFITH.

1892–1912, 2s. 6d. each. - General Index, 4s. net.

A JOURNAL OF EGYPTIAN ARCHAEOLOGY (issued Quarterly), commenced January, 1914. Vols. i–v,
6s. a part; Vol. vi (in progress), 12s. 6d. a part.

OFFICES OF THE EGYPT EXPLORATION SOCIETY: 13, Tavistock Square, London, W.C.
and 503, Tremont Temple, Boston, Mass., U.S.A.

Agents:

BERNARD QUARITCH, 11, GRAFTON STREET, NEW BOND STREET, W.;
HUMPHREY MILFORD, OXFORD UNIVERSITY PRESS, AMEN CORNER, E.C., AND 29, WEST 32ND STREET, NEW YORK, U.S.A.;
C. F. CLAY, CAMBRIDGE UNIVERSITY PRESS, FETTER LANE, E.C.;
KEGAN PAUL, TRENCH, TRÜBNER & Co., 68–74, CARTER LANE, E.C.; GEORGE SALBY, 65, GREAT RUSSELL STREET, W.C.

Lightning Source UK Ltd.
Milton Keynes UK
UKOW01f1900031017
310353UK00007B/437/P